I0605627

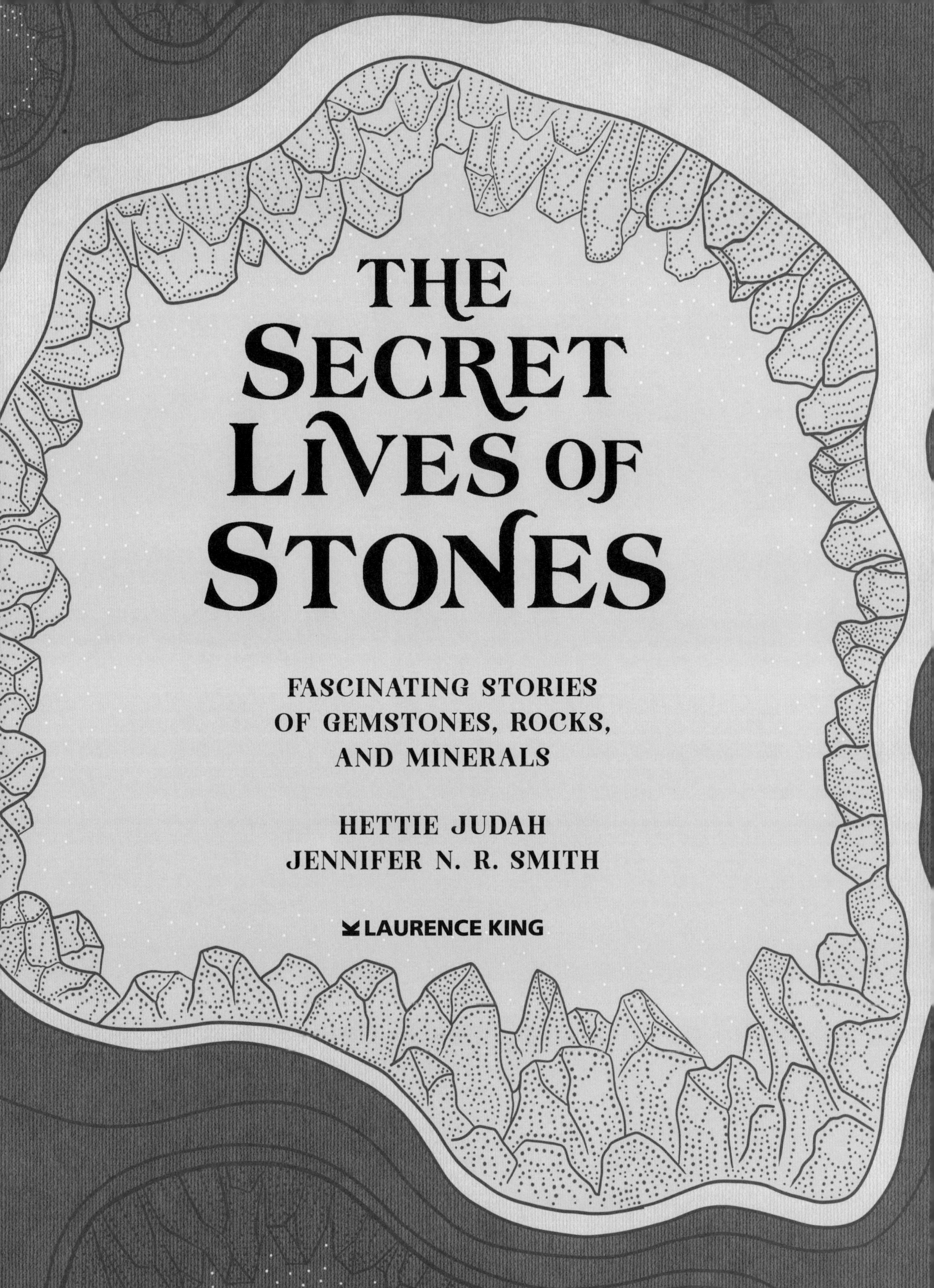

THE SECRET LIVES OF STONES

FASCINATING STORIES OF GEMSTONES, ROCKS, AND MINERALS

HETTIE JUDAH
JENNIFER N. R. SMITH

LAURENCE KING

For Ángel, Margot, and Scarlett—You Rock! H. J.

For the children who find treasure in the sediment of everyday. J. N. R. S.

LAURENCE KING
First published in the United States in 2025 by Laurence King

ISBN: 978-1-510-23134-4

10 9 8 7 6 5 4 3 2 1

Printed in China

Laurence King
An imprint of
Hachette Children's Group
Part of Hodder and Stoughton
Carmelite House
50 Victoria Embankment
London EC4Y 0DZ

An Hachette UK Company
www.hachette.co.uk
www.hachettechildrens.co.uk
www.laurenceking.com

Contents

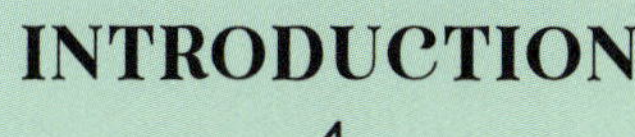

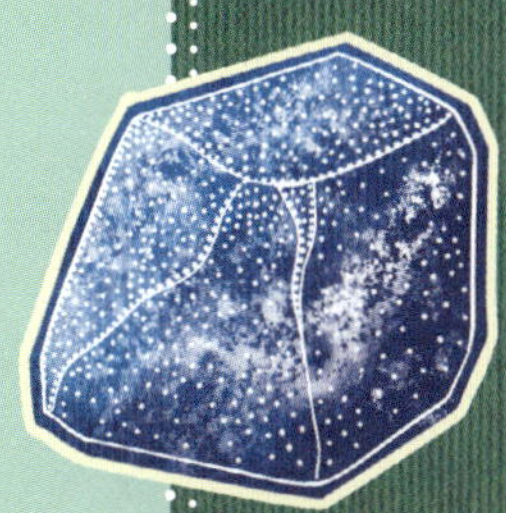

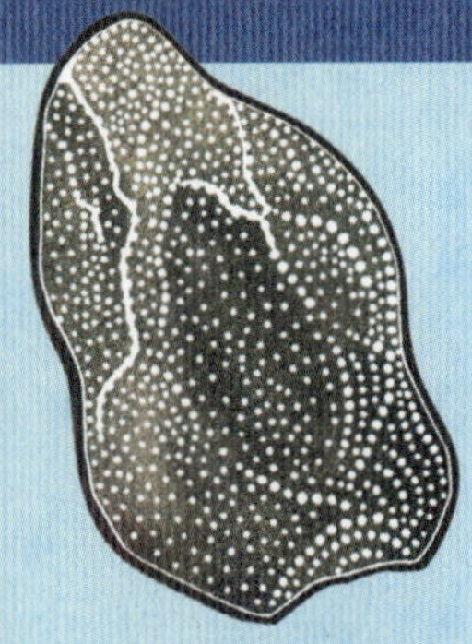

Introduction

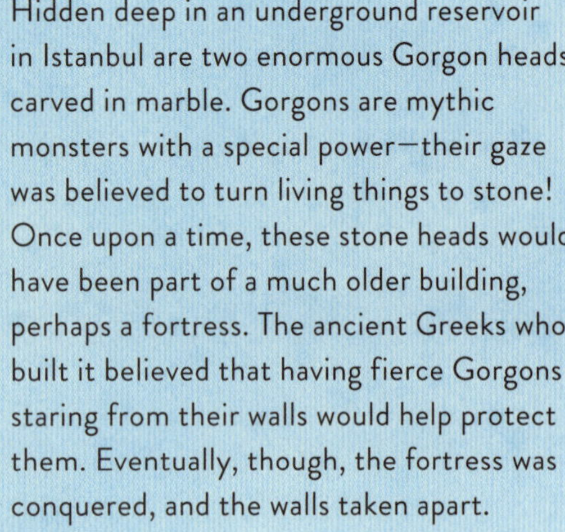

Hidden deep in an underground reservoir in Istanbul are two enormous Gorgon heads carved in marble. Gorgons are mythic monsters with a special power—their gaze was believed to turn living things to stone! Once upon a time, these stone heads would have been part of a much older building, perhaps a fortress. The ancient Greeks who built it believed that having fierce Gorgons staring from their walls would help protect them. Eventually, though, the fortress was conquered, and the walls taken apart.

It is hard work to carve and transport big blocks of stone, so parts of old buildings were often used to make new ones. When the Byzantine Emperor Justinian set about his grand building projects 1,500 years ago in Istanbul, he reused many stones from earlier structures. Among them were the Gorgon heads, which his architects used to form the base of pillars in a reservoir known today as the Sunken Palace.

I lived in Istanbul when my two sons were very young, and we'd sometimes visit the Sunken Palace. The Gorgon heads are the star attraction, and they still look spooky, even thousands of years after they were carved.

The Secret Lives of Stones looks at the mineral world in curious ways. All stones have a story, even those you might consider ordinary looking. Very often, that story tells us something about human history. The Gorgons in the Sunken Palace can help guide us through some of the themes linking the stories in this book. They can tell us interesting things about the relationship between stones, human culture, and the planet we live on.

The Gorgon heads are works of art. Humans have carved stone into artworks for tens of thousands of years. Stone is tough and slow to change, so carved stone objects are often the only evidence we have of civilizations from long ago.

The myth of the Gorgons is one of many stories from around the world inspired by stones. Rocks are found in the strangest shapes. Seen from a certain angle, they might look like people or even monsters. Oddly shaped rocks have inspired myths in which living things are turned to stone. Before people understood that dinosaurs once lived on Earth, stories of dragons and giants helped them explain the enormous bones and teeth they found.

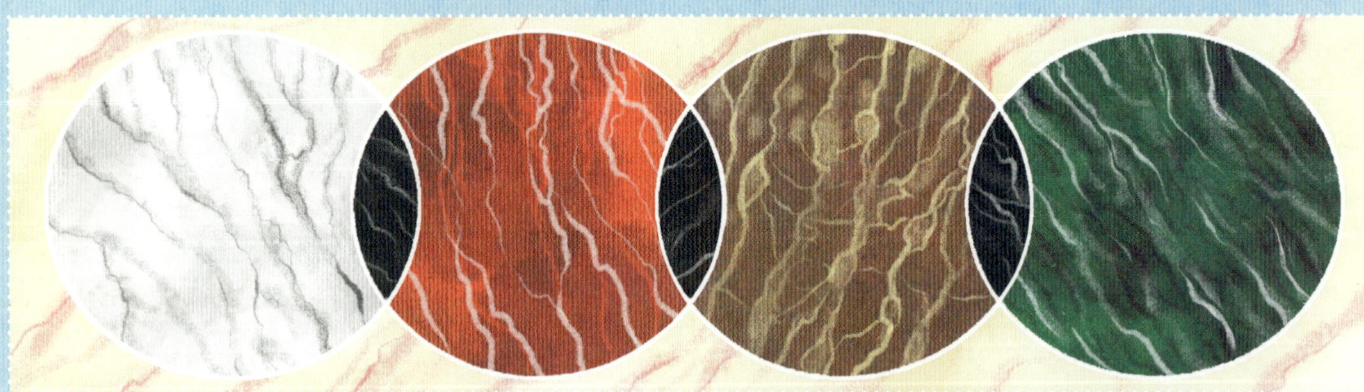

Humans' very earliest tools were stone: First, hammer stones to hit with, then axes and flints to cut with. The Gorgon heads are part of a long tradition of using stones as building materials.

Carvings of Gorgons—and in particular their mortal sister, Medusa—were very popular with the ancient Greeks. People carried small stone carvings of Gorgon heads to bring them luck, just as people today might carry a favorite crystal or pebble as a talisman. Most cultures around the world have stones that mark special places. Sacred stones are often associated with a holy person or with the spirits of the dead. There are also stones—such as crystal balls—believed to be capable of magic in the hands of those who know how to use them.

Stone also tells us stories about the history of our planet. The marble that was carved for the Gorgon heads is a metamorphic rock made hard and crystalline by powerful heat and pressure from within the Earth. Before it was turned into marble, it was limestone—a sedimentary rock that formed hundreds of millions of years ago at the bottom of an ancient ocean. Limestone is composed of the tiny fossils and shells of miniscule sea creatures. That means that the marble contains material that was once part of living creatures! So, the Gorgon heads really did have secret lives—though perhaps not the ones you expected.

Constructing magnificent buildings out of stone is a way that cultures express their power. Looking at ancient ruins we can see how power passed from one group to another. This is what happened to the Gorgon heads. Once part of a grand building constructed by the ancient Greeks, they were reused by the Emperor Justinian. Justinian's architects expressed his power by constructing even grander buildings, and they positioned the Gorgon heads upside down in the dark, almost as if they wanted to show them who was boss! Rulers also express their power through jewelry. Wearing precious gemstones is a way of displaying wealth while looking magnificent.

AMBER

Amber was once a sticky liquid called **resin**, which flows out of trees in the **conifer** family when they are cut. The resin hardens, much like a scab, protecting the bark from infection so that it can heal.

Trees that produce resin include cedar, fir, juniper, pine, redwood, spruce, yew, and larch.

In prehistoric forests, so much resin dribbled out of pine trees that insects and other small creatures often drowned in the sticky stuff! Over hundreds of thousands of years, the resin turned to stone, preserving the creatures inside. The oldest pieces of amber are 320 million years old, dating from the Carboniferous period. Some of the creatures that have been found preserved in amber lived long before the first dinosaurs!

Amber can range from dark red to milky white, but the classic color is deep gold. Today, amber is usually gathered from underground mines. There are also deposits of amber beneath the ocean. Amber is so light that it can be carried by salty water, and as a result there are certain beaches where it can be found washed up after storms.

Flowers, fungi, insects, spiders, crabs, and even a gecko have been found preserved in amber.

In the seventh century BCE, the Greek philosopher Thales of Miletus discovered that amber rubbed on animal fur attracted light objects such as feathers or dried grass, a phenomenon we call static electricity. The word *electricity* comes from the ancient Greek name for amber: *elektron*.

Amber was abundant on the beaches of the Baltic Sea in the old country of Prussia, and in 1699 the ruler of Prussia, Frederick III, had so much amber that he commanded his artisans to construct an entire chamber lined with it. He envisioned an amber room glowing like the summer sun in the Baltic winters. When Frederick III died in 1713, the chamber was still unfinished.

Frederick III's son washed his hands of his father's project by sending the amber room as a gift to Tsar Peter the Great of Russia. The chamber was completed in 1755 and installed in the Summer Palace. Almost 200 years later, during the World War II, the amber room was dismantled and stolen by the Nazis. It has since disappeared, becoming one of the world's greatest missing treasures.

Millstone grit

Millstone grit could win a prize for "most literal ever description of a stone." Its surface is **gritty,** like sandpaper, and it was indeed used for millstones in the past. Millstone grit comes from the north of England. It is a **sandstone** that runs under a high, wild kind of landscape known as moorland.

Sandstone is what's known as a "clastic" sedimentary rock. All those little gritty bits that fused to make this rock were once parts of an even older generation of mountains. They eroded over millions of years of rain, wind, and waves, and the granite particles were carried to the mouth of the ocean where they built up in the slow-moving water of a delta.

The sediment that formed millstone grit settled during the Carboniferous period, between 360 and 300 million years ago. This was then a tropical region—a strange thought for anyone who has walked in freezing winds and rain in the Peak District and North York Moors in England.

When did you last eat bread? Or noodles? Or pancakes? All have been eaten by humans for thousands of years, and all are made from grains. To make these foods, grain must have its tough outer layer removed before being crushed to make flour.

The earliest grain store ever found was over 11,000 years old. Shaped pieces of rock called saddle stones were found here—they had a shallow dip to hold grain, which would have been ground with a handheld stone. Portable saddle stones were the earliest mills, used by cultures from Mexico to Mongolia.

The Romans designed bigger millstones to increase grain production. A dome-shaped stone went underneath, and a millstone fitted over it. Grain was poured through a hole in the millstone and ground by the movement of one stone against another. More than thirty large mills have been found at Pompeii—these would have been turned by teams of mules or people enslaved by the Roman Empire.

Thank goodness for the watermill! In a watermill, the power of running water pushes paddles, which turn the millstone to grind the grain. The Romans introduced early watermill designs to Britain. Some of the first millstones in Britain would have been carved in millstone grit.

A millstone needs to be very tough. You don't want the stone getting ground down and leaving chips of grit in your flour. It needs to have a rough surface so that it catches grains as though it is chewing them. The flour produced by gritstone milling is coarse. When white bread became fashionable, people no longer wanted the coarse, gray stuff. Thousands of old millstones are scattered around the moors. There are so many that the Peak District National Park has a millstone as its emblem.

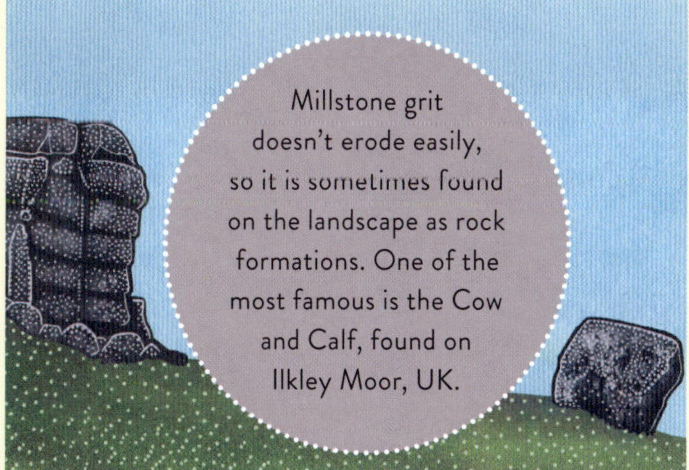

Millstone grit doesn't erode easily, so it is sometimes found on the landscape as rock formations. One of the most famous is the Cow and Calf, found on Ilkley Moor, UK.

Pumice

You may already have seen pumice in your home. This stone can **float** in water and is so **rough** that it is used to smooth hard skin. People often rub their feet with it after a long soak in the bath.

The burning hot cloud of pumice, gas, and ash that pours out of an explosive volcano is known as a pyroclastic flow. A pyroclastic surge is similar but contains more gas and less pumice.

Pumice is full of little holes and air bubbles. It looks like solid foam. Magma can carry huge amounts of dissolved gas, which is released as it rises toward the surface of the Earth. The effect is like a bottle of cola being shaken—as the pressure builds, the lava explodes as a froth of molten rock. As the foam flies, it hardens into pumice.

Explosive volcanoes spew out material so violently that their craters can collapse. Burning clouds of pumice, gas and ash can travel across landscapes at speeds of more than 62 miles per hour (mph). The largest recorded explosive eruption on land was at Mount Tambora in Indonesia in 1815. The cloud of pumice, gas, and ash was so powerful that it traveled 25 miles (mi) out over the sea and made the water boil.

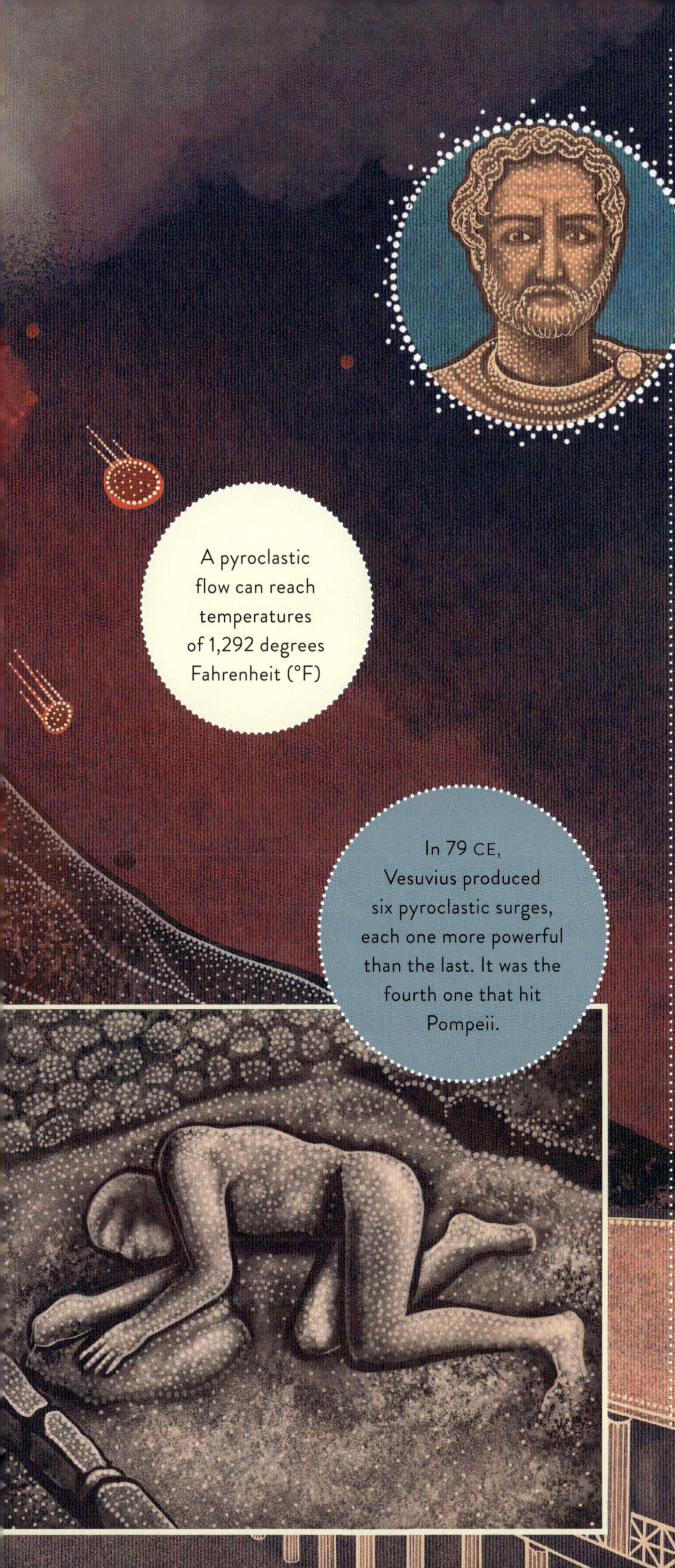

The most powerful explosive eruptions are known as "Plinian" in honor of the Roman author, Pliny the Younger. He wrote the first detailed account of an explosive volcano in action. In 79 CE, Pliny the Younger was staying on the Bay of Naples with his uncle, a natural historian known as Pliny the Elder. When Vesuvius erupted on the other side of the bay, they had a perfect view.

Seeing a cloud of unusual size and shape emerge, Pliny the Younger compared it to an umbrella pine. That's how the ash looked as it burst up out of the crater. Pliny the Elder took a boat across the bay to get a closer look.

As he drew closer, the falling ash got hotter and hotter and was gradually replaced by a storm of pumice. After climbing off his boat, Pliny the Elder visited his friends and reassured them that all would be alright, then went to sleep. He was woken up by the building shaking as the courtyard started filling up with hot ash.

Pliny the Elder and his friends quickly tied pillows to their heads for protection and left. Shortly after walking to the shore, Pliny the Elder collapsed and died, most likely due to sulfuric fumes from the volcano.

Things were even worse on the other side of Vesuvius. The city of Herculaneum had been destroyed the night before. Hot ash then covered the city of Pompeii, where the inhabitants experienced a sudden heat surge that took the temperature to more than 482°F, causing instant death. Buried beneath hot ash and mud, both Herculaneum and Pompeii were preserved for centuries as they were at the moment they were hit by the eruption.

TUFF

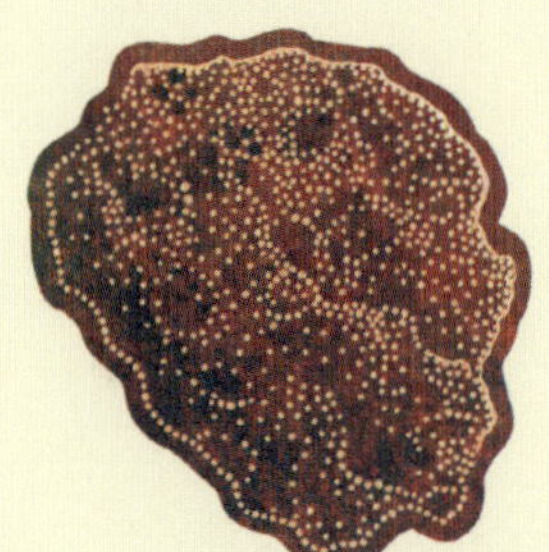

An erupting volcano ejects **ash** made up of rock fragments, mineral crystals and volcanic glass. This hot material fuses into little clumps known as **lapilli**, which fall to Earth like hailstones. Tuff is formed from a thick layer of **welded lapilli**. It is, for stone, **soft** and easy to carve.

On April 5, 1722, boats led by the Dutch explorer Jacob Roggeveen arrived at a remote island in the southeastern Pacific Ocean. Roggeveen named it "Easter Island" to mark the date of his arrival, Easter Sunday. The inhabitants already had their own name for the island: Rapa Nui.

Rapa Nui is famous for its sacred ancestor statues known as moai (pronounced mo-eye), which are carved from tuff. They are towering figures with angular heads and domed bellies. Most of the hundreds of moai around the island are about 13 feet (ft) tall, though some are even bigger.

Rapa Nui was once divided between different clans, each of which erected high stone platforms called ahu, along which their moai were arranged in rows facing inland. Once in position, some moai had a ball of red scoria (a foamy-looking stone) positioned on their head to represent long hair wound in a ball, and white coral placed in their eye sockets to make them look alive. They would have been an imposing sight.

Rapa Nui was once home to lush tropical forests, but after more than a thousand years of human habitation, all of the trees were felled to make buildings and canoes. Archaeologists think that the islanders used the trees to transport the enormous stone carvings. Using stout ropes, each clan would have worked together to drag an enormous statue on rollers made from tree trunks from the quarry to their ahu.

Rapa Nui is just the tip of a 9,842-ft-high volcanic cone! Because of this, the stone available on the island is volcanic. Obsidian (volcanic glass) was used to make cutting blades, and hard basalt was used for heavy tools. Tuff was used for the moai, which were all carved at the same quarry. Tuff is rough, coarse, and hard to the touch. It is pitted with little holes and looks almost spongy. When they were first carved, the moai would have been a sandy yellow color.

Marble

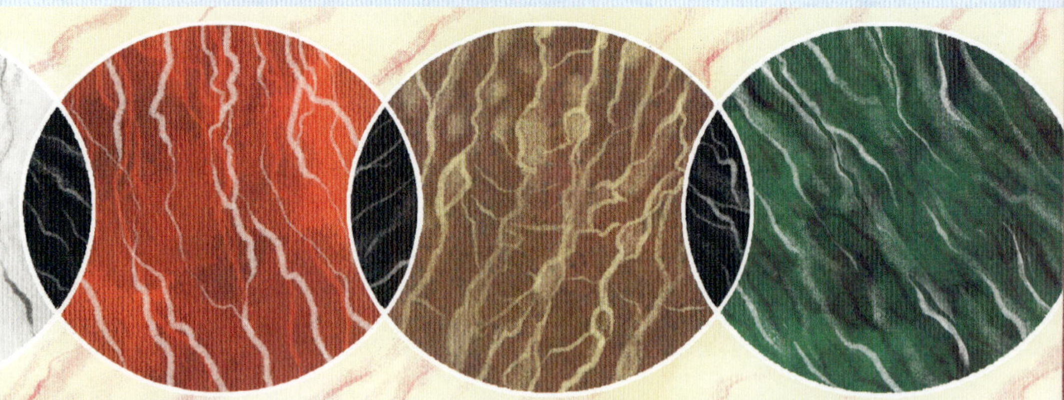

Most famous in **white**, marble can be found in a rich variety of colors, including deep **reds**, **browns,** and even **greens**. You can often identify it by thin streaks in the stone, which are described as "veins." If you touch marble, you will find that it is cool and smooth. If you tried to lift it, you'd find it tremendously heavy.

Today, marble is popular as a decorative stone for grand buildings, so keep an eye out for it, because you might see it in a building near you, on the floors, or walls, or fireplaces. For many thousands of years, it has been used by artists and architects to communicate power and sophistication. Not only is it a beautiful stone, but marble is also particularly hard and durable.

The ancient Greeks first used marble for building temples. The temples on the islands of Paros and Naxos were made from local white marble that sparkled in the sun. It looked so dazzling that every city in Greece that could afford it wanted marble from Paros or Naxos for their temples, too.

The Greeks discovered other sources of marble. Some 2,500 years ago in Athens, the magnificent Parthenon temple was constructed in marble from nearby Mount Pendelikón. The Parthenon was decorated with carvings illustrating mythological battles designed by the sculptor Phidias which included warriors wrestling centaurs and gods fighting giants. The figures in Phidias's sculptures were as perfect as he could imagine them, with smooth skin and bulging muscles. Phidias's designs for the Parthenon influenced the way human bodies were sculpted for thousands of years.

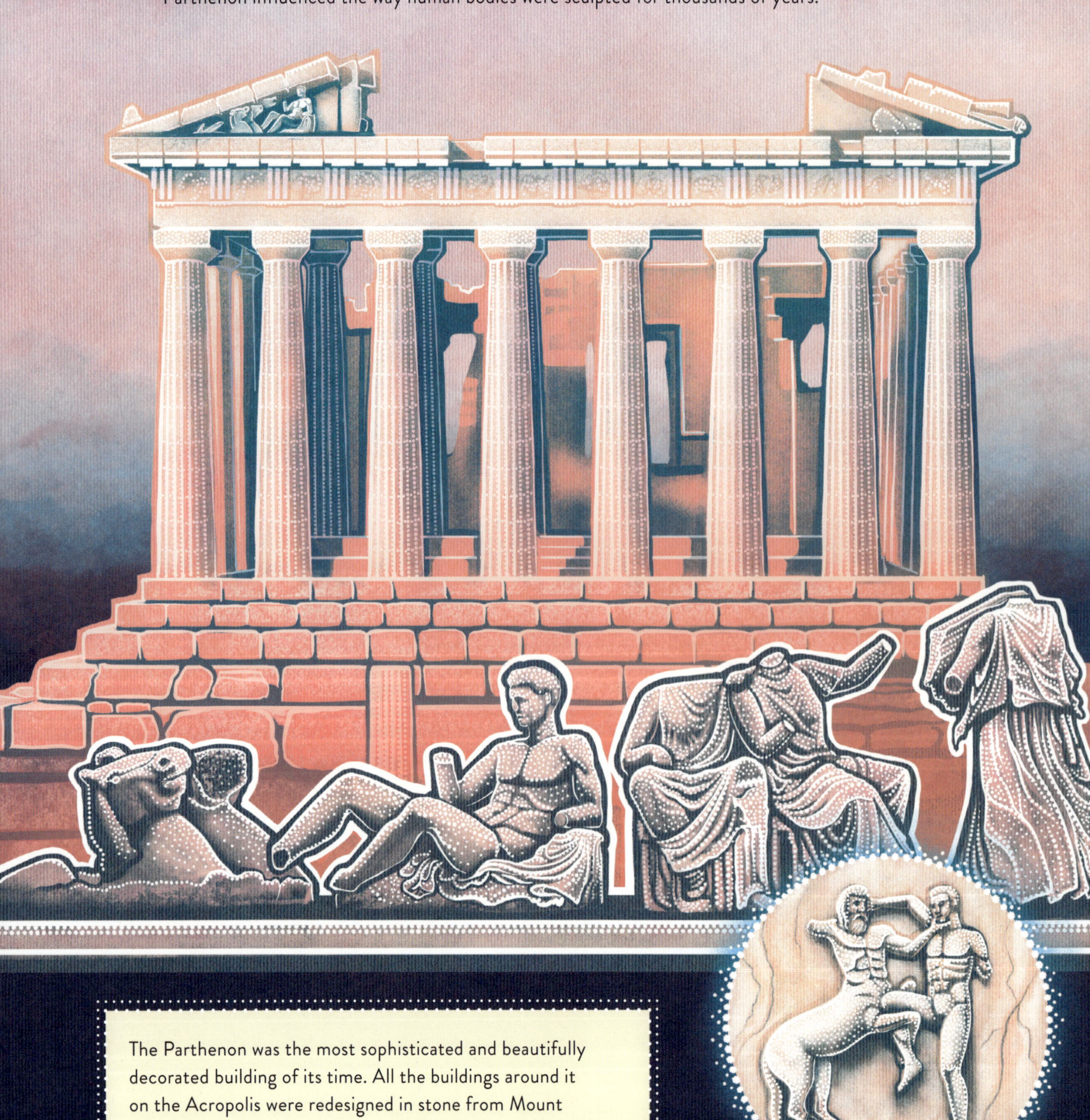

The Parthenon was the most sophisticated and beautifully decorated building of its time. All the buildings around it on the Acropolis were redesigned in stone from Mount Pendelikón to match, until the citadel of Athens glowed a brilliant white.

Marble is metamorphic rock that is transformed by tremendous pressure. Greek marble started as sedimentary limestone formed beneath the ancient ocean Tethys. Over many millions of years, as the continental plate of Africa moved, colliding and sliding under Eurasia, Tethys shrunk, and the limestone got squeezed until some of it formed marble.

Although the marbles used in the traditional children's game are glass, long ago they would have been rounded pieces of clay or polished stones, hence the name.

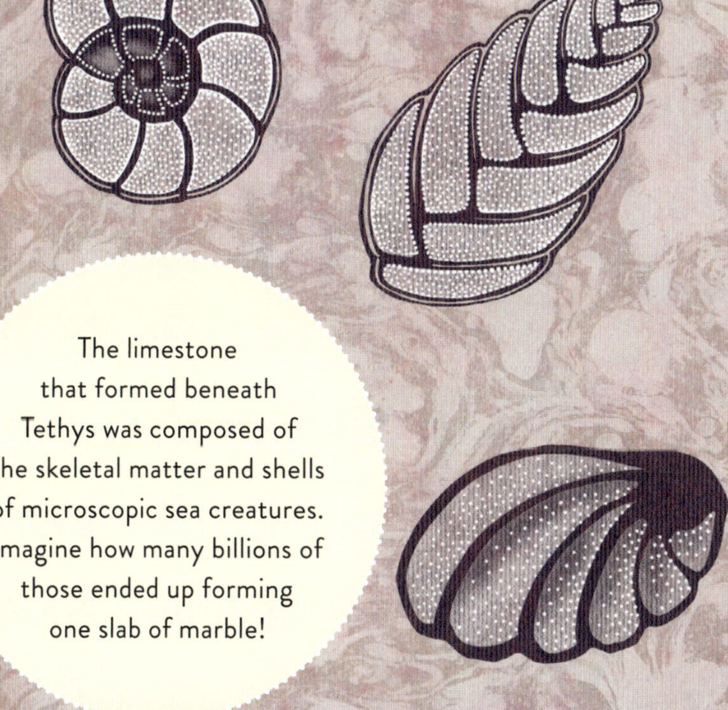

The limestone that formed beneath Tethys was composed of the skeletal matter and shells of microscopic sea creatures. Imagine how many billions of those ended up forming one slab of marble!

The ancient ocean Tethys is named after a Titan from Greek mythology. Tethys was mother to the river gods and the nymphs of the ocean.

Emerald

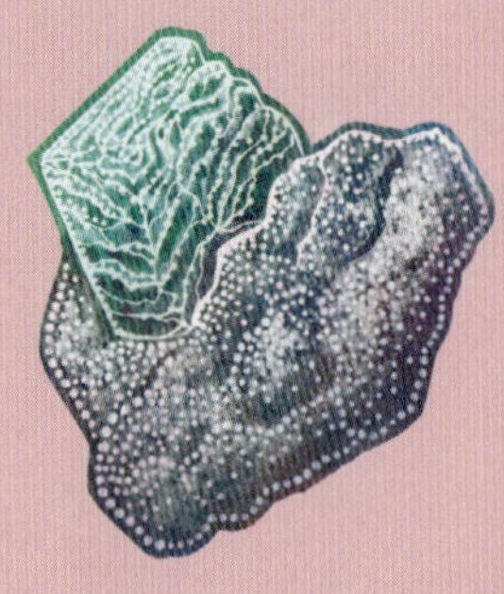

Emerald is an intense **green** variety of a mineral called **beryl**. It is a prized gemstone, much **rarer** than diamond. Emeralds are found in greens from olive to deep pine, with variations in color caused by traces of the metals chromium, vanadium, and iron. The finest emeralds are very deep green with just a hint of blue from iron. Like all gemstones, the most sought-after are the largest and clearest. Since emeralds are relatively **soft** and almost all have some visible impurities, clear emeralds of a good size are particularly valuable.

Emerald is mined at only a few sites around the world. The most celebrated source is in Colombia in South America, where emeralds have been prized for centuries. Today, the largest emerald mine in the world is in Zambia in southern Africa.

It is also possible to create emeralds in a laboratory: They are known as synthetic emeralds and are still valuable, but not as valuable as emeralds from a mine.

In the Inca civilization of South America, emeralds were worshipped. In the 1500s, the Spanish invaded the Inca Empire and stole emeralds from their temples. Searching for the source of the gems, the conquistadors seized the mines in what is now Colombia and shipped emeralds to Europe in vast quantities.

There are many varieties of beryl. A pale, watery blue beryl is known as an aquamarine. In bright yellow, beryl is known as heliodor, and in pale pink it is called morganite.

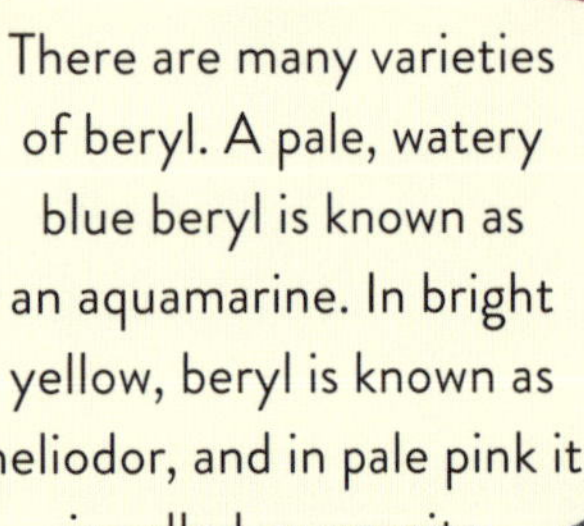

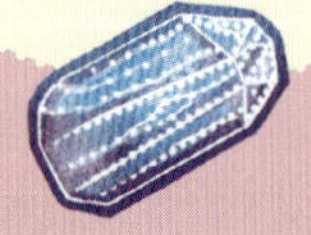

One of the most famous emeralds was an enormous crescent-shaped stone owned by Anita Delgado. She was a maharani in northern India, and the emerald was a gift from her husband Jagatjit Singh, a wealthy maharaja. She had asked him for the stone after spotting it among the jewels decorating his oldest elephant. The emerald had come from Colombia in South America, brought centuries earlier by Spanish and Portuguese merchants.

Anita was born in Spain in 1890. Her parents were poor café owners in the city of Málaga, and as a teenager, Anita worked as a dancer at a cabaret in the capital city Madrid. In 1906, royalty from around the world traveled to Madrid for the Spanish King's wedding. Jagatjit Singh was among the guests, and during his trip he visited the cabaret. Romantic legend has it that he fell in love with Anita at first sight.

Jagatjit Singh gave Anita the great crescent emerald on her nineteenth birthday as a reward for learning Urdu. "Now you own the moon," he told her, "but I don't believe you will be able to wear it." Left alone with the jewel, she slipped gold thread around the two peaks of the crescent and arrived at her party with the emerald at her forehead. She described the gem as her lucky charm.

JADE

Jade is a waxy-looking stone and is most prized in shades of **green**, from pale cucumber to bright broccoli. It may look like a tasty vegetable (and is often carved to resemble one) but do NOT try to eat it: Jade is exceptionally **hard**! Modern jewelers shape jade with diamond-tipped drills.

Fu Hao is the first-known female general in Chinese history.

Associated with purity, nobility, and immortality, the ancient Chinese considered jade more precious than gold, and because it is so tough, it carried associations of long life. For the ancient Chinese, it also represented a physical connection to their ancestors — jade carvings would often be passed down through many generations. The tomb of the Bronze Age warrior queen Fu Hao, who died around 1200 BCE, contained the largest collection of Chinese jade ever excavated. The 755 pieces buried with Fu Hao included a flat pendant of a phoenix, carved figures of tigers, elephants, and dragons, and a seated woman with the tail of a fish.

The jade treasure tells us that Fu Hao was powerful and wealthy. Her tomb was more than 23 ft deep, and she was buried with six dogs and sixteen servants, who would have been sacrificed to accompany her into the afterlife.

The word *jade* refers to two different stones: nephrite and jadeite. They share many qualities. Both are exceptionally hard, milky in appearance, and found in a variety of colors, the most prized of which is green. Jadeite was beloved of the Maya people of Central America. Chinese jade is nephrite.

Nephrite jade is also treasured by the Maori of Aotearoa (New Zealand), who historically used the stone for jewelry and ceremonial weapons.

The use of jade in royal burials became more and more elaborate. By the Han period 2,000 years ago, members of powerful Chinese families were buried in full suits of jade made from many pieces of stone wired together. This armor would have been too heavy for a living person to move in and was there for protection in case they needed to battle evil spirits after death. Beneath the armor they had jade plugs placed in their body's cavities to preserve them from decay.

Turquoise

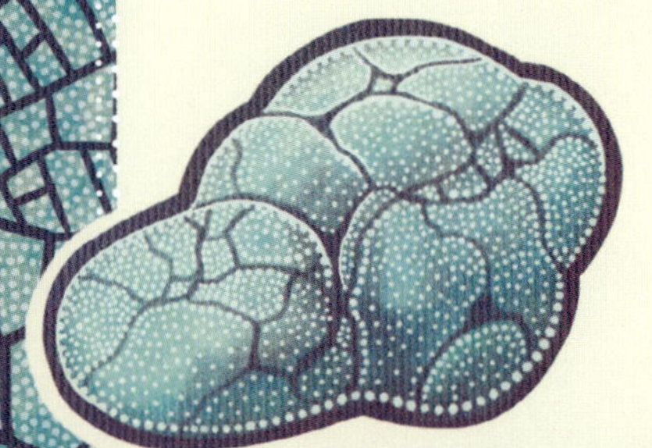

Bright **blue-green** turquoise was popular in many ancient civilizations. The blue color is caused by **copper**. If you look carefully, you might find an old building with a copper roof near you. You will see that the surface is a similar bright bluish-green color where the copper has been exposed to damp air. Turquoise is a **soft**, **opaque** stone. Stones with particularly heavy patterns of veins are known as spiderweb turquoise.

The Aztec civilization founded the city of Tenochtitlan in 1325, at a site they were led to by their god of war, Huitzilopochtli. He had told them to settle where they found an eagle on a cactus eating a snake. The Aztec people called themselves "Mexica" and their empire occupied part of present-day Mexico.

The Mexica believed the sun was made of turquoise and decorated many sacred objects in thin layers of blue mosaic. They used turquoise to cover effigies and masks of Huitzilopochtli, who was said to carry a mighty fire serpent as a weapon—a terrifying creature with turquoise skin. Turquoise tesserae (the tiny tiles used to make mosaic) decorated the handles of ceremonial stone knives used by priests for ritual sacrifices, during which human hearts were offered to the sun god! Turquoise and gold offerings were also thrown into sacred bodies of water.

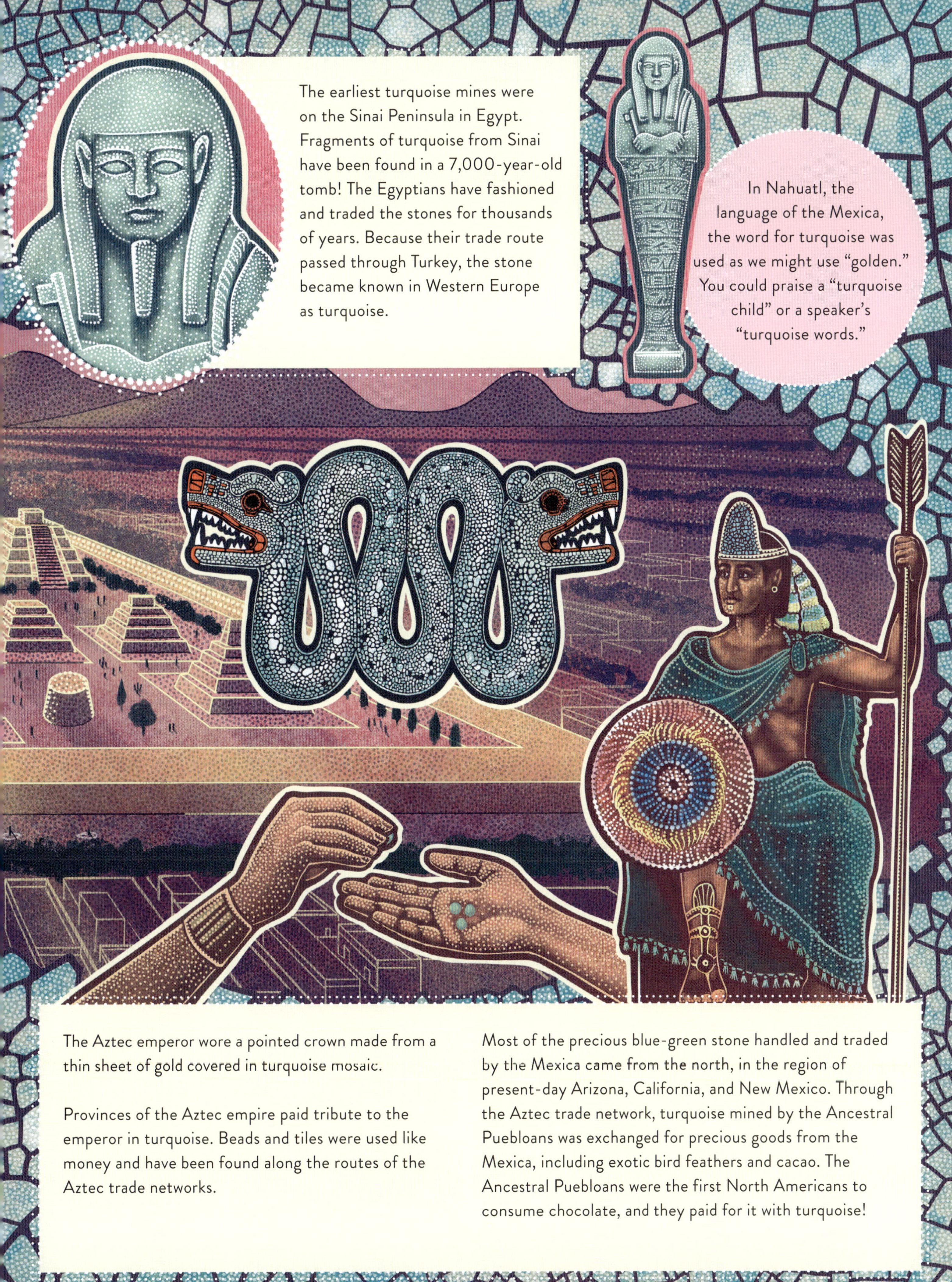

The earliest turquoise mines were on the Sinai Peninsula in Egypt. Fragments of turquoise from Sinai have been found in a 7,000-year-old tomb! The Egyptians have fashioned and traded the stones for thousands of years. Because their trade route passed through Turkey, the stone became known in Western Europe as turquoise.

In Nahuatl, the language of the Mexica, the word for turquoise was used as we might use "golden." You could praise a "turquoise child" or a speaker's "turquoise words."

The Aztec emperor wore a pointed crown made from a thin sheet of gold covered in turquoise mosaic.

Provinces of the Aztec empire paid tribute to the emperor in turquoise. Beads and tiles were used like money and have been found along the routes of the Aztec trade networks.

Most of the precious blue-green stone handled and traded by the Mexica came from the north, in the region of present-day Arizona, California, and New Mexico. Through the Aztec trade network, turquoise mined by the Ancestral Puebloans was exchanged for precious goods from the Mexica, including exotic bird feathers and cacao. The Ancestral Puebloans were the first North Americans to consume chocolate, and they paid for it with turquoise!

Lapis lazuli

For thousands of years, this intense **blue** stone has been polished for jewelry, carved into figurines, or thinly sliced to decorate ornaments. Many different **minerals** make up this wonderful blue stone—as a result, the appearance of lapis lazuli can vary; stones mined in Chile and Russia, for example, are often speckled or banded with white.

Like the night sky, lapis lazuli sparkles with stars, thanks to little flecks of iron pyrite—a mineral also known as "fool's gold."

The word *lapis* means "stone" in Latin, so the name translates simply as "blue stone."

Lapis lazuli is rare. The most famous source is in Afghanistan, and it has been mined in this mountainous region for more than 6,000 years.

Lapis lazuli was beloved of the ancient Egyptians, who used it for carvings of scarab beetles and beaded jewelry. They even crushed it into powder to use as makeup. The stones would have been brought to Egypt by Sumerian merchants who had carried it along trade routes from Afghanistan more than 1,864 mi away.

A royal burial chamber from ancient Mesopotamia became known by archaeologists as the Great Death Pit at Ur. It is thought to be the burial chamber of Queen Pu-abi. The royal corpse wore a fine golden headdress decorated with lapis lazuli and stones of red carnelian.

The Sumerians produced the earliest work of literature—a poem called the "Epic of Gilgamesh."

The story starts with Gilgamesh, the ruler of the city of Uruk.

He became selfish and arrogant, so the gods decided to teach Gilgamesh a lesson. They created the wild man Enkidu to fight him.

After the fight, Enkidu and Gilgamesh unexpectedly become best friends, annoying the gods even more.

The opening verses of the "Epic" make clear how important the poem was to the Sumerians. They describe it as being carved into the most precious material imaginable at the time: Lapis lazuli!

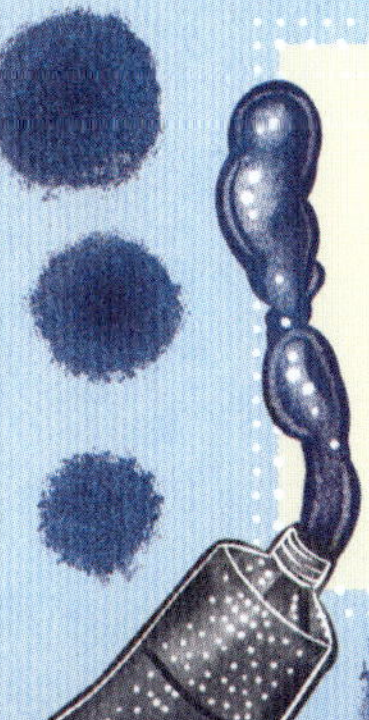

Until the nineteenth century, ultramarine paint took its color from lapis lazuli. Artists' assistants would grind chunks of lapis lazuli into very fine powder, purify it, then mix it with egg yolk, milk, or plant gum. Due to the rarity of lapis lazuli and the difficulty of extracting the pigment, ultramarine was *very* expensive. During the Italian Renaissance, it was used to paint only special subjects, such as the robes of the Virgin Mary.

AMETHYST

Quartz in every color of **purple**, from pale lavender to dark plum, is known as amethyst. The color comes from traces of **iron** in the crystal, which is turned purple by natural radiation in the surrounding rock.

Amethysts are often found in geodes. These are rounded formations lined with crystals that have slowly built up inside cavities in volcanic rock formed by gas bubbles long ago.

Geodes are the size of the cavity they have grown in—some are small enough to hold in your hand, while others are as tall as you!

The word *amethyst* is said to derive from the Greek *amethustos*, which means "not drunken." Crystal mystics thought that the ancient Greeks believed amethyst allowed people to drink wine without getting drunk. But there is no evidence that the ancient Greeks believed any such thing!

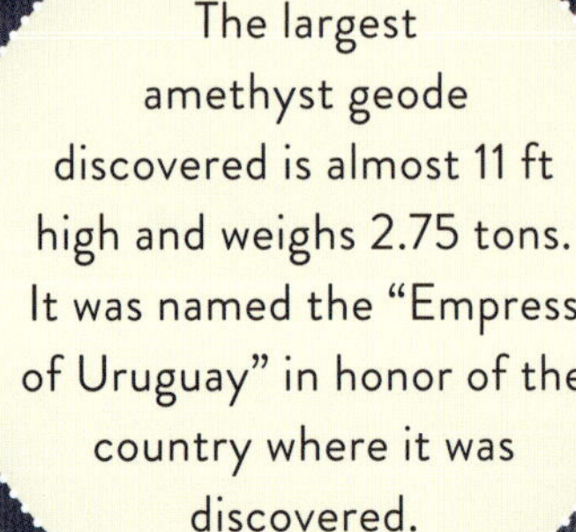

The largest amethyst geode discovered is almost 11 ft high and weighs 2.75 tons. It was named the "Empress of Uruguay" in honor of the country where it was discovered.

During the 1970s, many groups of young people chose to live very differently to their parents. Some called them hippies, though this was not a word they used themselves. Instead, they might have said they were followers of a "New Age" movement because they wanted to work toward a new age of love and peace. They studied different forms of spirituality and developed their own religious rituals. As New Age ideas became popular in the 1970s, demand for amethyst boomed. Crystal lovers believed that amethysts and other stones were charged with special mystical powers that could alter people's moods or treat a variety of illnesses.

Mystics within the New Age movement attributed magical qualities to crystals. Some believed that this purple stone could absorb negative forces and even transmit violet rays from the planet Mercury. Many of these ideas came from ancient books about stones known as lapidaries, some of which are thousands of years old and full of myths and folklore. Healing crystals are still popular, and billions of dollars are spent on them every year.

Amethyst is found around the world and exported in large quantities from Brazil, Uruguay, and Bolivia in South America, and Zambia in Africa. Mining amethysts can be a dangerous business.

In 1992, the small Brazilian town of São Gabriel changed its name to Ametista do Sul—"Amethyst of the South." So many crystals were mined in the region that it declared itself the amethyst capital of the world. The interior of the local church sparkles with 44 tons of amethyst.

OPAL

There are precious and not-so-precious opals, and there are common opals, too, known as "potch." Precious opals have a quality called "play of color"—they look as though **rainbows** are trapped inside. The range in color from **milky white** to **black**, laced with reds, oranges, greens, blues, and violets.

The not-so-precious opals are **fire opals**. These clear stones are found in warm colors that range from pale orange to flaming red, with little or none of the "play of color" effect.

Opals are found in hot places, including the Australian desert and mountains of Ethiopia. Amazingly, they take their fiery brilliance from water—but you can't crack an opal and see liquid dribble out: The water is deep in the stones' structure. Most of the opal is made of little spheres of silica, like teeny tiny glass balls. It's this that creates the play of color.

When Minnie Berrington first saw opals poured on a desk, she was desperate to try mining them herself. At age twenty-eight, in 1925, a taste for adventure had taken her from a dull job in London to a new life in Australia. Her brother worked trucking goods into the Australian bush. Minnie traveled with him and listened to tales of the opal fields. At that time, all the opal miners were men, but that didn't stop Minnie. Along with her brother, she visited the famous opal fields at Coober Pedy (pronounced koo-buh pea-dee). It was here in a post office set up in a cave that she watched the assistant postmaster pour fiery opals on his desk. That day, Minnie and her brother bought mining rights and started digging.

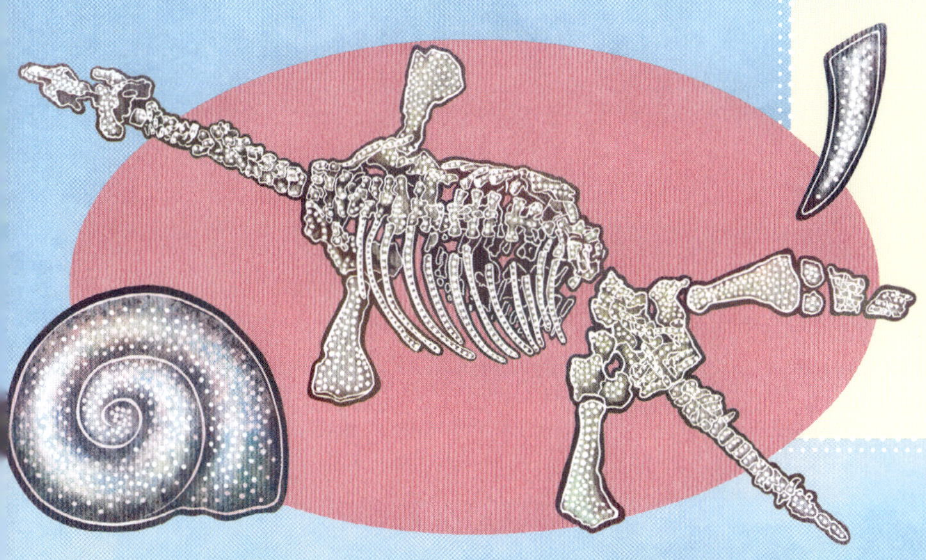

Sometimes opal forms in gaps left by plants and animals, creating opalized fossils. Miners in Australia have found beautiful opalized snails. The most famous opal fossil is a pliosaur found at Coober Pedy. He's known as Eric and is displayed at the Australian Museum in Sydney. Not only have Eric's bones been opalized, but also the contents of his stomach—opalized, half-digested prehistoric fish.

The most valued opals are black opals, mined near the town of Lightning Ridge in New South Wales, Australia.

Opal is the national gemstone of Australia.

Life in Coober Pedy was tough. In summer, the temperature rose to 104°F. Miners dug with pickaxes and shovels, and winched soil out in leather buckets. Minnie's brother soon gave up, but she stuck at it.

In 1930, the photographer Emil Otto Hoppé traveled to Australia. He was used to photographing aristocrats and celebrities, but in Australia, he wanted to photograph everyone. Amid all the heat and dust, Hoppé was very surprised to find a young woman in a neat coat with a fur collar sitting outside the local shop with a whole sheep carcass hanging behind her. (The carcass would have been cut up, weighed, and sold for meat). He was fascinated by Minnie and took her portrait—she looks strong, mischievous, and bright eyed. Hoppé titled it: "Minnie Berrington, the only woman on the Coober Pedy Opal Fields."

DIAMOND

Do you believe a gem can carry a **curse**? The Victorians did, and they couldn't get enough of cursed diamonds in detective novels, ghost stories, and spooky plays. Books about great diamonds tantalized readers with romance, wealth, and gruesome tragedies. You can understand why people love these stories—it is deliciously tempting to believe that wicked secrets lie behind wealth and power.

Many great diamonds really do have strange histories. Some have been stolen—both by force and cunning—many times. Until the late nineteenth century, most diamonds came from India. Those that made their way to Europe were often rumored to carry a curse.

One of India's most important diamonds was the Koh-i-Noor, which weighed a massive 186 carats. For centuries, it was an emblem of powerful rulers.

In 1849, at the end of the Second Anglo-Sikh War, it was surrendered to Queen Victoria by Duleep Singh, the ten-year-old Maharaja of Punjab.

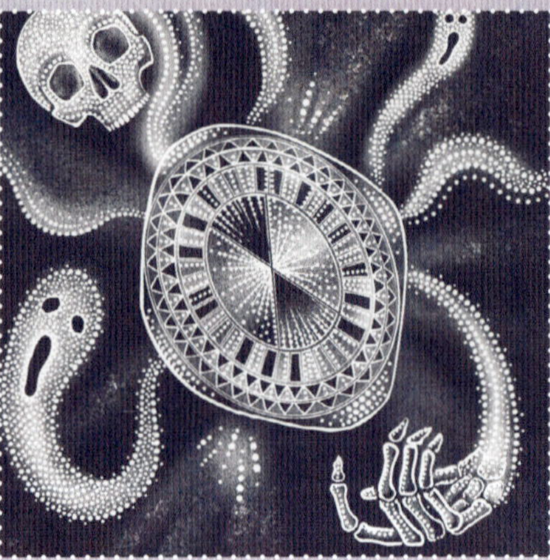

Stories circulated that the stone brought misfortune. This did not deter the Royal Family.

Queen Victoria's husband Prince Albert had the Koh-i-Noor recut to make a sparkling jewel.

Koh-i-Noor now sits in a crown made for Elizabeth, consort of George VI, for her coronation in 1937.

Gem dealers used the craze for cursed diamonds to drum up publicity. In 1910, a dark blue diamond weighing 45.5 carats was advertised in the *New York Times*, accompanied by an outrageous, bloodthirsty "history."

According to this "history," the first dealer to bring the diamond to Europe was said to have had his throat ripped out by dogs.

Before his death, the dealer sold the diamond to French King Louis XVI, who went on to be beheaded with his wife, Marie Antoinette, during the French Revolution. Other owners of the blue diamond became ill or suffered mysterious deaths.

Most of these stories were nonsense, but they attracted attention. The blue diamond sold for $18,000, becoming the property of heiress Evalyn Walsh.

She loved spooking people with rumors of the diamond's curse and flaunted it at parties. At one party, she hung it from the collar of her Great Dane dog.

Terrible things really did happen to Evalyn Walsh—her children died young, and her husband had severe mental health issues. Although none of that could be blamed on a diamond, no one wanted to take a chance on it again. Now known as the Hope Diamond, it has been on display at the Smithsonian Museum in Washington, D.C., since 1958.

Diamond is the hardest known natural substance. It's a clear mineral composed entirely of carbon, formed at high temperatures under tremendous pressure hundreds of miles down in the mantle of the Earth.

Although best known as a colorless stone, diamonds are found in many colors, but the most prized is pale rose pink.

A raw diamond could be mistaken for a pebble if you didn't know what to look for. They must be cut to create the illusion of inner fire.

The stones are carried to the surface by volcanic activity, rising through the mantle and crust with magma. Geologists hunting for diamond deposits search for a rare volcanic rock called kimberlite, which forms enormous cones in the craters of dead volcanoes.

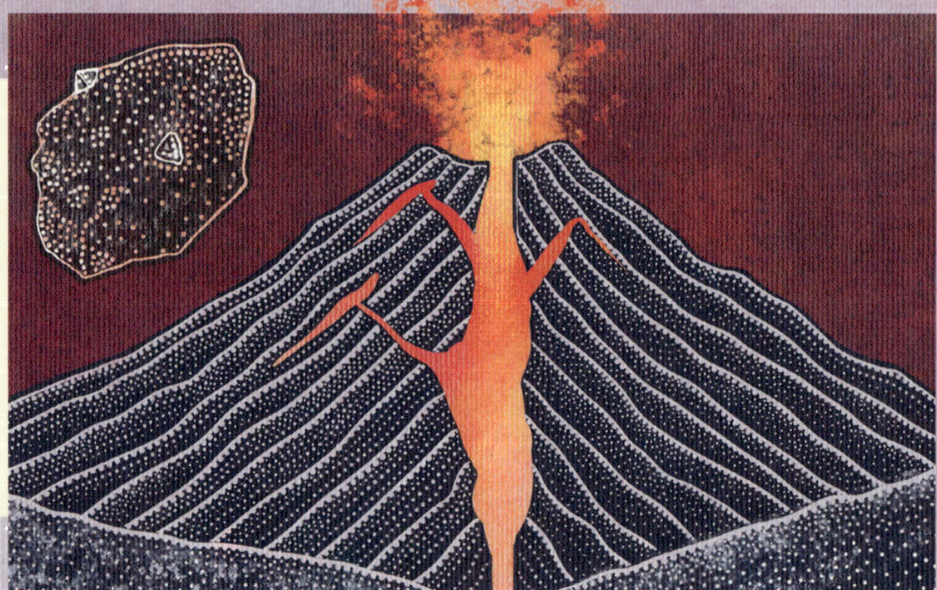

Diamonds have only been mined from the Earth for 150 years. Before that, they were found in deposits brought to the surface in volcanic eruptions. Until recently, India was the world's main source of diamonds, and they were very rare. Only the very rich owned diamonds. That changed in 1871 when diamonds were found on a farm in Kimberley, South Africa. This led to diamonds being mined in tremendous volumes, making them more affordable. The mine in Kimberley is so famous that kimberlite was named after it. Over the years, it yielded 14.5 million carats of diamonds.

The weight of diamonds is measured in carats. One carat is 0.007 ounces (oz).

Diamonds have a peculiar quality — they stick to fat! This led to a legend known as The Valley of the Diamonds, first told in the fourth century and so well known in the medieval world that it has been found in manuscripts from Europe to China. It was said that the floor of a deep crevasse in India was lined with magnificent gems. The sides were too steep to climb, so gem hunters threw chunks of fatty meat down instead. When eagles swooped down to get the meat, diamonds would stick to the fat. The gem hunters could then pluck the diamonds from the eagles' nests!

Moon Rock

On July 16, 1969, the Apollo 11 space mission launched from Cape Canaveral in Florida, USA. The crew's mission was to land on the Moon, gather material, perform a few experiments, and record the first human steps for TV audiences back on Earth. On July 20, the Lunar Module, piloted by Commander Neil Armstrong and Edwin "Buzz" Aldrin, landed on a large dark plain known as the Sea of Tranquility.

The distance between Earth and the Moon increases by 1.49 inches (in) every year.

When the Moon first formed, it was only 15,534 mi away from Earth. Today it is 238,855 mi away.

One of Aldrin and Armstrong's most important tasks was to gather material from the Moon's surface. Using special rakes, they collected 48.5 pounds (lb) of Moon rock, including two core samples from 5 in below the surface.

Scientists were very excited about the Apollo 11 mission. One of the biggest questions they hoped it would answer was how the Moon formed and what its relationship was to the Earth.

In 1975, scientists William Hartmann and Donald R. Davis first presented their radical theory on the origin of the Moon. It became known as the "big thwack" hypothesis, which has since been formally accepted by lunar experts as the Moon's origin story. It goes like this: Shortly after the formation of the Earth 4.5 billion years ago, when the planet was still a seething, molten mass, it suffered a slight collision with a much smaller planetary body. The little planet got smooshed, and there was a colossal explosion of liquid rock. The heavier stuff reformed back into the Earth, but a great cloud of debris was left flying around—it was this material that formed the Moon.

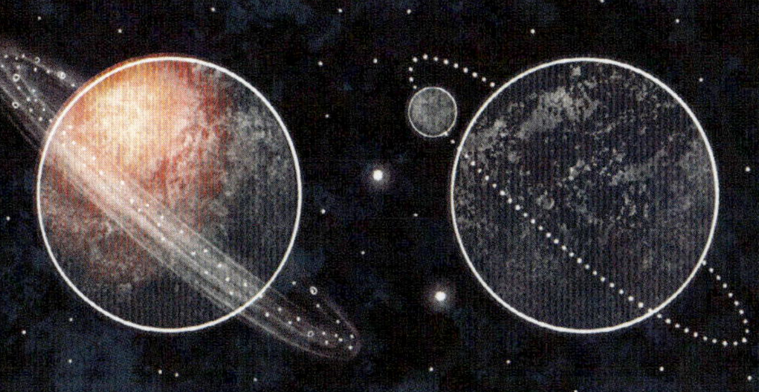

The term *Moon rock* sounds quite impressive, but actually, most of the material brought back from the Moon was what geologists call regolith—dust and bits of loose, broken rock that littered the surface.

Analyzing the Moon rock, scientists discovered several things. First, almost all the samples were igneous—they had formed from hot molten rock. There was also some metamorphic rock on the Moon: Stone that had been transformed by the heat and pressure of meteorite bombardments.

Second, there are almost no minerals on the Moon that contain water in their structure. Third, the Moon is much less dense than Earth and lacks our planet's massive iron core.

Analysis also suggested that Earth and the Moon formed at the same distance from the Sun.

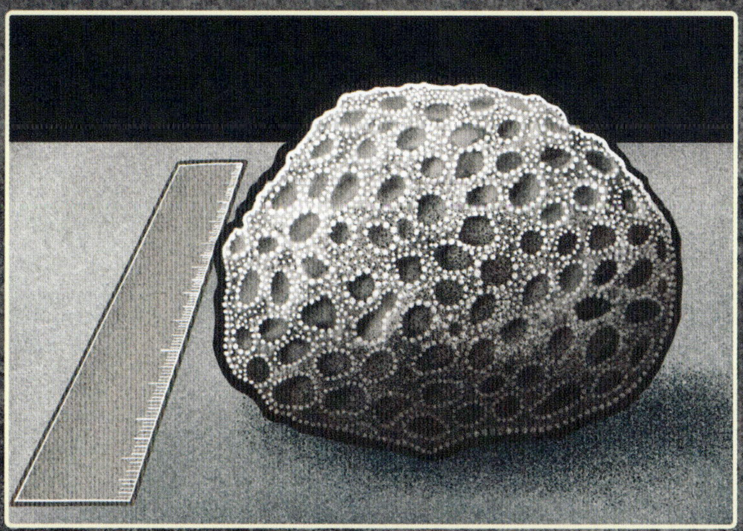

FLINT

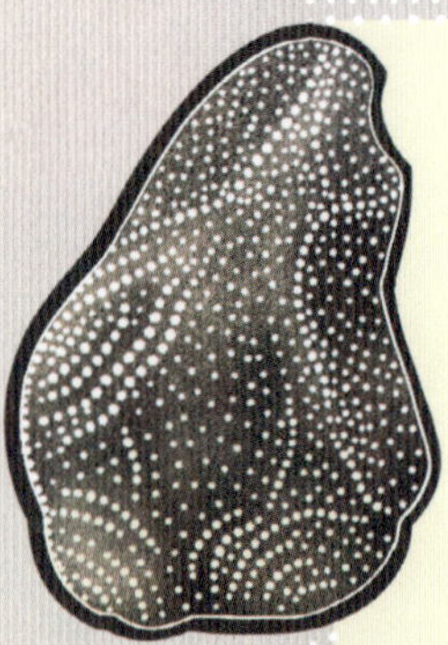

You can find flint in the weirdest shapes. Flint is often found in chalk or limestone, and the rounded nodules can look like bones or body parts. The outside of the flint nodule will be white or light gray, but the inside is **dark**. Thin slivers of flint are a little translucent—you can see some light through them. Flintlike stone that is paler gray, or brown and milky, is known as **chert**. The difference in color is caused by microscopic particles of air or water in the stone—otherwise, flint and chert have the same properties.

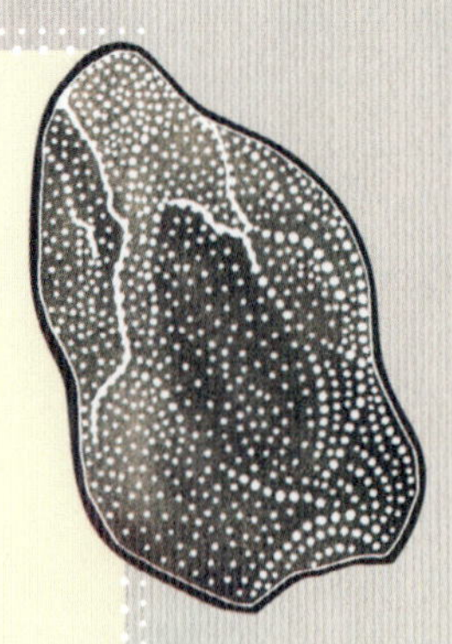

Flint is formed from silica that was part of sea creatures, such as sponges and plankton, that lived more than 60 million years ago! It is a sedimentary form of quartz. Because they are harder than the surrounding sedimentary rock, flint nodules are revealed by erosion. If a limestone or chalk cliff is worn away by crashing waves, for example, flint and chert will often build up beneath it, forming pebbles.

Flint and other stones were the first human tools: As a result, this early period in human history is known as the Stone Age. The first tools were simple hammers—any strong stone that felt comfortable in your hand. Two-and-a-half million years ago, in East Africa, humans started chipping off thin stone flakes to sharpen them into cutting tools. Over hundreds of thousands of years, stone tools became more specialized. Hard stones were chipped or ground into ax-heads, while long flaked pieces became knives. Scrapers were made to remove fat and blood from animal hides, and blades were set in wooden handles to make harpoons, spears, and arrows.

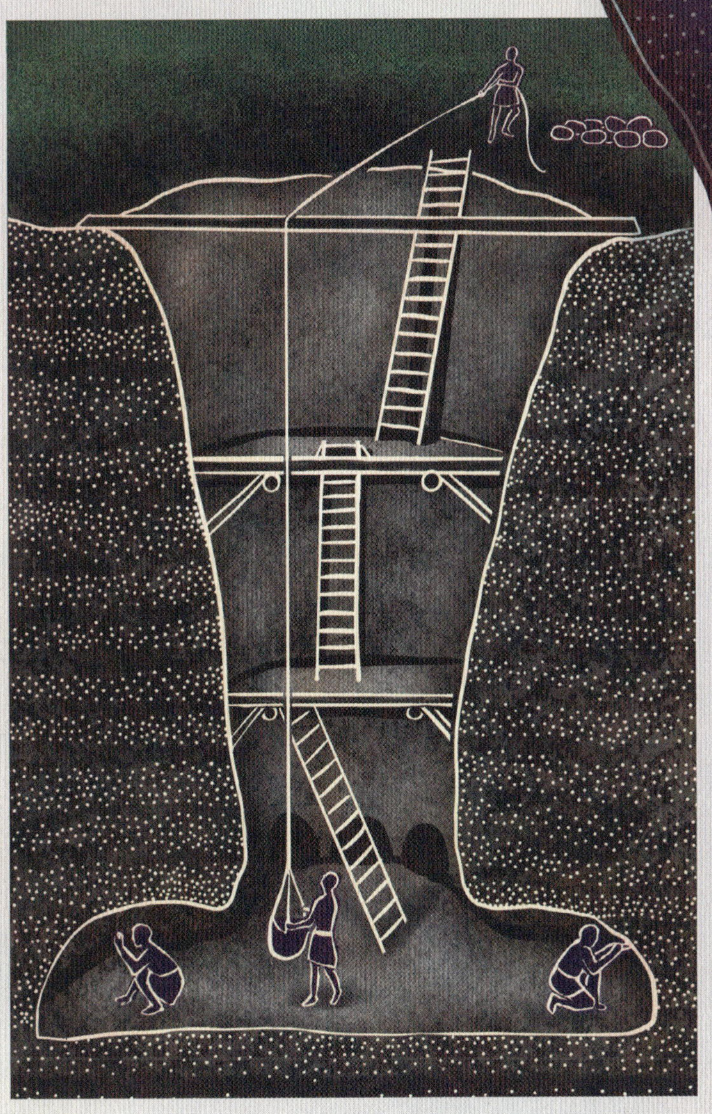

By the late Stone Age, whole complexes rose up to dig for and form stone tools. In the east of England, the gloomily named archaeological site Grime's Graves is not a grave at all, but the location of a prehistoric flint factory. There are 400 pits there, first dug for flint about 5,000 years ago.

The Stone Age started 3.4 million years ago and lasted until about 4,000 years ago and the adoption of bronze tools. In other words, for most of human history, we've been in the Stone Age. Until very recently, flint was still being struck against pieces of steel to start fires, used in early firearms called "flintlocks" and as a building material.

The Victorians loved collecting ancient objects — both fossils and stone tools. One of the greatest forgers of the time was the mysterious Flint Jack. He became very skilled with flint and made arrow heads and other tools that he sold as archaeological discoveries. Hundreds of forgeries by Flint Jack were purchased by British museums. He invented completely new shapes for flint tools—including fishhooks—which really confused historians at the time. They thought they'd discovered evidence of a new culture!

SARSEN

One of the greatest celebrities of the rock world is Stonehenge—a formation of raised banks, ditches, and standing stones that has been a site of human activity for more than 5,000 years. Stonehenge sits on Salisbury Plain in England, and the huge stones that form its famous standing circle are sarsens that were raised into position 4,500 years ago.

Stonehenge is built from two different kinds of stone. The smaller inner ring of the monument is made of darker bluestones, which were brought all the way from the Preseli Hills in South Wales, 150 mi away.

Because this monument was built long before written history, no one knows for certain what its purpose was. The first history book to mention Stonehenge was written by Geoffrey of Monmouth in 1136. He described how the stone monument had once stood in Ireland, and that the stones had been uprooted and transported to Salisbury Plain by Merlin the magician. Geoffrey thought that Stonehenge was a memorial for noble men who died in battle.

Today, archaeologists believe Stonehenge was a sacred site where burials and other rituals were performed. The sarsens were arranged to mark the movement of the Sun. A single standing stone, known as the Heel Stone, lines up with the rising Sun on the longest day of the year, known as the summer solstice. On the shortest day of the year—the winter solstice—the Sun can be seen setting between the stones of one of the great trilithons, where two upright stones carry a third across the top to resemble an arch.

Stonehenge is not the only ancient monument on Salisbury Plain. There are traces of ancient structures dotted across a huge area: Clearly, this was a very important place for the Neolithic and Bronze Age people. The village of Avebury is home to a wide ring and long avenue of standing stones.

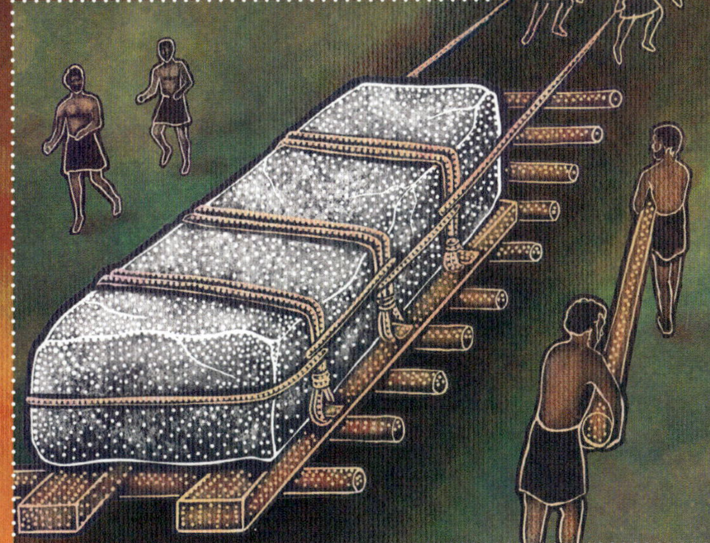

There are artificial hillocks made from sarsens, chalk, and earth built to house the remains of the dead. In England, these burial mounds are known as barrows. One of the most famous is the West Kennet Long Barrow near Avebury. On one of the sarsens at the entrance to the Long Barrow, you can see marks where people sharpened their flint ax-heads 5,000 years ago!

Archaeologists have recently discovered that the sarsens used in the construction of Stonehenge came from near Avebury. Each of the 27.5-ton stones would have been dragged on wooden rollers 19 mi across Salisbury Plain. The stones were hauled into position in deep ditches using strong plant fiber ropes and wooden frames, then packed in place with stones and earth.

The sarsens are all that remains of a thin layer of sedimentary rock that formed from sandy silt 35 million years ago, when the chalk landscape was covered by a tropical wetland. Because the layer of sandstone above the chalk was thin, it gradually eroded and broke up into large boulders. Today, most of them have been removed for use as building materials, but for thousands of years the sarsens held extraordinary significance for the inhabitants of ancient Britain.

Coal

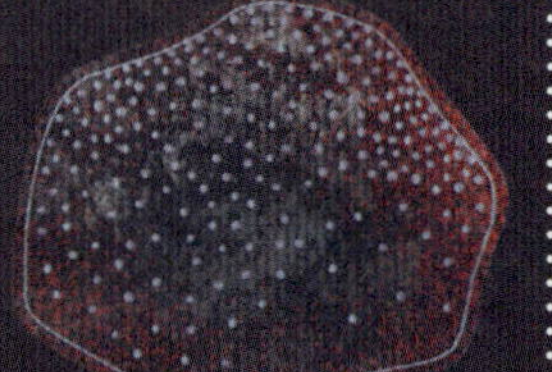

Coal is rock that is more than 50 percent **carbon** by weight. The more carbon it contains, the more heat is produced when it burns. The most valuable coal is called **anthracite**, which is 95 percent carbon. Like gasoline, coal is a fossil fuel.

You probably know that coal is formed of ancient plant matter, but did you know that no new coal is forming? The creation of coal was a one-off event that required special conditions—a permanently wet tropical region and huge chasms in the earth. The conditions that created coal occurred between 360 and 300 million years ago during the Carboniferous period. This was an era of swamps and soaring prehistoric trees, of the first little reptiles and absolutely enormous insects—dragonflies in the Carboniferous had a wingspan of up to 28 in!

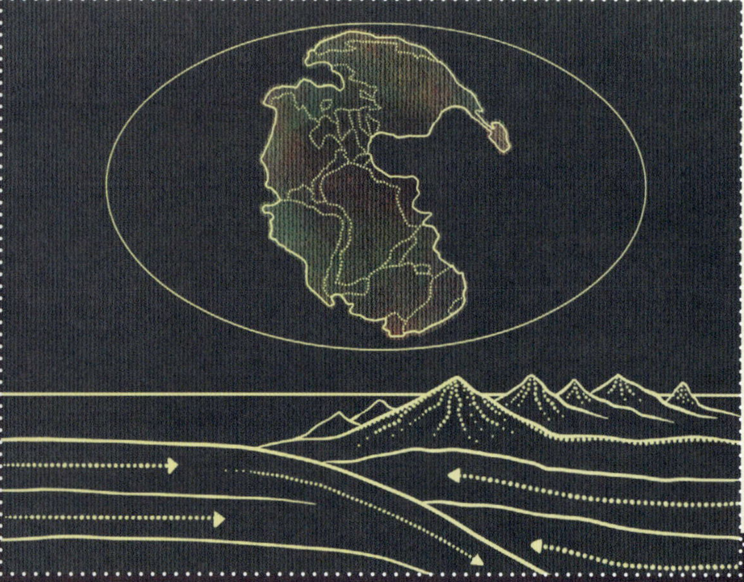

Over Earth's long history, the continental plates have moved at an exceedingly slow pace, sometimes colliding, sometimes drifting apart. At times, so many landmasses collided that they formed a supercontinent. The most recent of the seven supercontinents was formed during the Carboniferous period. It is known as Pangea and was composed of almost all the landmasses on Earth. The slow collision of landmasses threw up massive mountain ranges, but around those mountains chasms and gaps appeared.

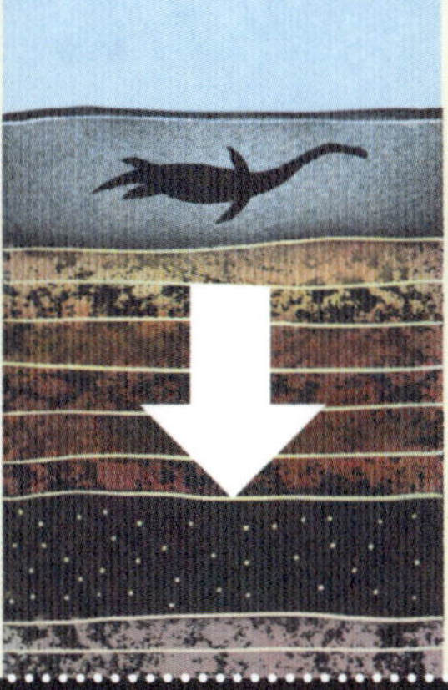

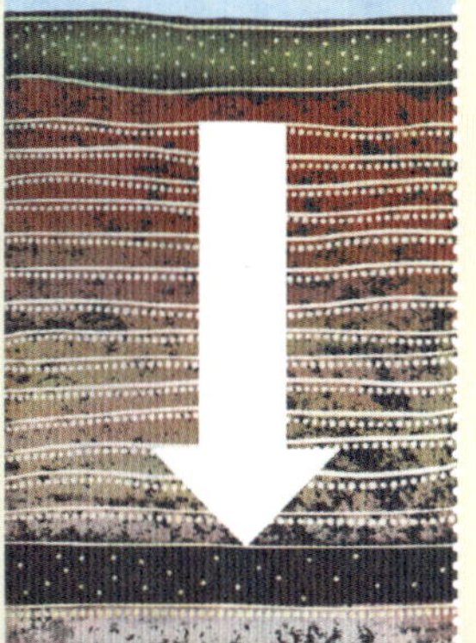

These chasms were very slowly filled with plant matter. The wet, swampy conditions offered protection from the bacteria and fungi that would have rotted the plant matter on land. The remains of those great mountain ranges pushed up during the formation of Pangea include the Appalachians in the United States. They are also some of the world's most important coal mining regions.

Coal played a starring role in the Industrial Revolution in Britain, thanks to the invention of the steam engine. The first working steam engine was built in 1712—it was not a vehicle but a machine that pumped water out of mines. People used coal to heat their homes and ovens, blacksmiths needed it to run their forges, and it was gobbled up by the new steam engines, too.

By the early nineteenth century, the first steam-powered vehicles were created. In 1825, George Stephenson designed the first passenger train, which ran between Darlington and Stockton in the north of England. Stephenson's most famous design was Rocket—it could travel at 36 mph.

In the years that followed, railroad networks were built across Britain, Europe, and the United States. Coal-powered engines allowed enormous numbers of people to travel and changed manufacturing in the nineteenth century.

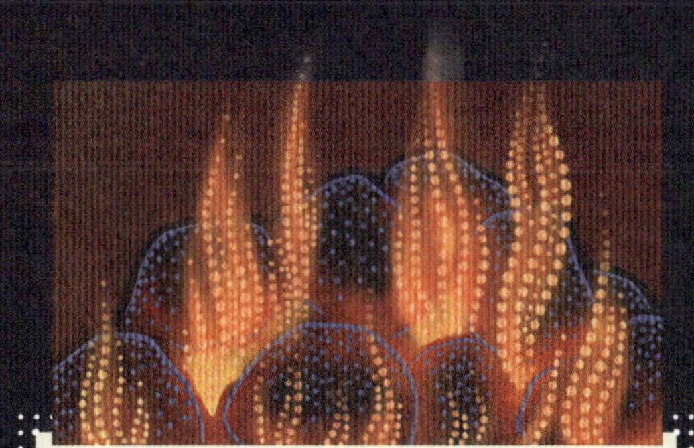

Mining coal pollutes the earth and water. Burning coal then releases long-buried carbon into the atmosphere. Rapid climate change caused by human activity started with the Industrial Revolution. Although you probably don't burn coal in your home, it is still used to generate electricity all over the world.

Coltan

Columbite-tantalite, or coltan, as it is more commonly known, is a **dull**, heavy, gray-black **ore**. Ore is a rock that contains a large amount of desirable mineral; the most valuable minerals are usually metals.

Coltan is often gathered by independent miners, who dig small pits and extract material with hand tools.

The most important sources of coltan are the Democratic Republic of the Congo, Rwanda, Nigeria, Brazil, and China. The composition of coltan varies, but the element that makes it so sought-after is the metal tantalum. Tantalum is strong, and when made into fine wire, very flexible. It is also an excellent conductor. This has made tantalum particularly valuable to the electronics industry. Many gadgets have a tiny quantity of tantalum in them, including smartphones, laptop computers, tablets, and games consoles.

Coltan is not the only rare mineral in demand. A group of seventeen metals known as rare earth elements are some of the most sought-after substances on Earth. These metals are used in modern computers and smartphones, as well as electric cars and wind turbines. This puts any country that has a good supply of these metals and can process them into a very powerful position. Currently, China supplies 95 percent of the world's rare earth elements.

The story of coltan is one example of how new technology can create a sudden demand for a mineral and the unexpected consequences this can have. The launch of the Sony PlayStation PS2 in the year 2000 was a big moment in the history of gaming. Fans started lining up outside the Tokyo store four days ahead of the launch. The PS2 became the most popular games console of all time, with 158 million sold around the world. After the launch of the PS2, the value of coltan leapt.

In the Democratic Republic of the Congo, this bump in value caused a gold-rush type frenzy known as coltan fever. Students dropped out of schools, farmers left their crops, and entire communities started digging for the valuable ore. At the time, the region was caught up in the Second Congo War. Money from selling coltan was used to fund the violence on both sides. More than 5 million people died by the end of the war in July 2003. The battle to control the trade in coltan and its profits earned this terrible conflict a memorable nickname: The PlayStation War.

Lodestone

Lodestones are naturally **magnetic** pieces of the mineral **magnetite**. Magnetite is metallic and dark—almost black—and can form **crystals** with eight or twelve sides. It is an oxide of **iron**, a chemical compound containing both iron and oxygen, found in igneous rock formations. Magnetite is a common mineral and one of the most important sources of iron.

Naturally occurring lodestone in large quantities can have a catastrophic impact on ships' compasses. It is very hard to navigate around a landmass that carries large deposits of lodestone!

The compass is one of the "Four Great Inventions" from ancient China that are said to have changed the world. Magnetic compasses are attracted to Earth's magnetic poles. If a piece of iron is rubbed on lodestone, it also becomes magnetic. It can then be balanced to show its natural attraction to the South and North Pole.

Confusingly, not all magnetite is strongly magnetic. Only strongly magnetic pieces of magnetite are lodestones.

The earliest compasses in China were used for fortune-telling rather than navigation! During the Han dynasty, about 2,000 years ago, stubby round-bottomed spoons were balanced at the center of charts surrounded by symbols.

The little lodestone spoon swung on its rounded base, pointing its handle south.

An expert who knew how to read the symbols could then work out the best position for a building, or the time and place for a special event.

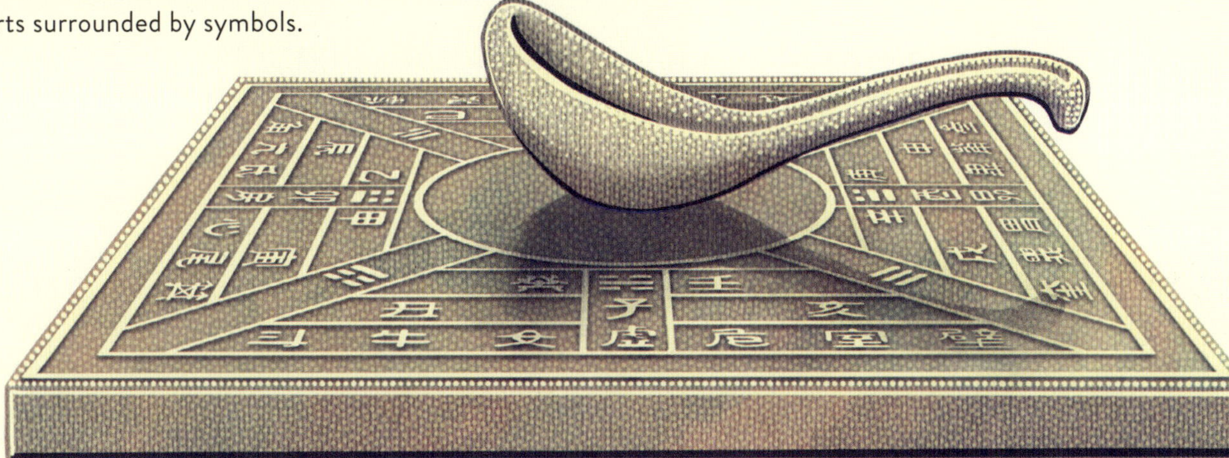

In the twelfth century, Chinese sailors started using compasses for navigation. They would insert magnetized needles into small wooden fish. The fish either floated in a bowl of water or hung from silk threads. In both positions, they were free to swing and point to the South Pole. Compasses made it easier for sailors to travel out of sight of land and find their way across great distances, allowing China to start trading with the Islamic world.

It was probably Islamic merchants who first introduced the compass to sailors in the Mediterranean. There is some disagreement about this, however. A statue on the Amalfi Coast in Italy honors a man named Flavio Gioia for inventing the compass in the year 1300. It is possible that the magnetic compass was developed in Europe just as it was first used by Chinese sailors. However, the first mention of a compass in a European science book was in 1187, so it was certainly not "invented" in 1300. As for Flavio Gioia—did he even exist? The compass needle of history currently points to "no."

There have been amazing cultures able to navigate by the sky and waves. The Polynesians undertook huge voyages in the Pacific Ocean without compasses, as did the Vikings in the Atlantic. For cultures without this knowledge, the arrival of the compass changed their relationship with the ocean. European compass needles pointed north rather than south. They had a round face decorated with the directions of the eight winds of the Mediterranean.

Since sailors no longer had to rely on the sun and stars for navigation, journeys—and wars—were possible all year round. Trade increased, and voyages of discovery were undertaken. The wide adoption of the compass truly opened the way for global exploration and all that followed, for good and ill.

The magnetic poles are not exactly positioned at the North and South Poles. Sailors learned that the closer they traveled to the poles, the less accurate their compasses became.

Navigation is the process of figuring out your location and then following a route. Before the compass, if sailors were out of sight of land, they navigated by studying the waves, sun, or stars.

Pele's Hair

Pele is the Hawaiian goddess of the volcano. She and her family are not distant creator figures—they are the land itself. Hawaii Island is home to four active volcanos. Pele's flowing lava body has both creative and destructive power, adding layers of basalt rock to the island but also capable of burning everything in its path. The legends of Pele and her family are told through poems, dances, songs, and stories, and offerings of flowers and food are left near the volcanic crater that forms her home. As a volcano goddess, Pele is known for her explosive temper.

Magma is the name for lava before it reaches the surface of the Earth.

The people of Hawaii have lived alongside volcanoes for centuries. Their land is full of power and energy; it changes and feels very alive. Because the people of these islands have such deep understanding of volcanic activity, geologists use Hawaiian terms to describe different kinds of flowing lava. The crust of the flowing basalt lava called pāhoehoe (pronounced pa-ho-ee ho-ee) is quite smooth and forms twisting shapes like thick rope or wrinkly elephant skin. It makes a hot, crackling, tinkling sound as it moves. A rough, stony crust that looks like a pile of burning coals is instead called ʻaʻā.

Obsidian is another form of volcanic glass.

The composition of lava varies, but it always contains a large quantity of the mineral silica. More than half the mass of the Earth's crust is silica. It's the material used to make window glass. Have you ever seen a movie of someone blowing glass? This will give you an idea of the texture silica has in its hot liquid form. Silica makes magma sticky, and it influences the way a volcano behaves. If the magma contains more silica, it will get stuck in the crater, making the volcano violently explosive. If the magma contains less silica, it will flow easily—volcanoes with flowing lava are called "effusive" volcanoes.

Because it contains so much silica, lava that cools rapidly can form volcanic glass. When flowing lava bubbles up or squirts like a fountain, strands are sent flying through the air creating glass formations called Pele's hair and Pele's tears. Pele's hair is needle-fine—the trails of fast flying lava. Pele's tears are the droplets that formed at the end of these strands, and they really do look like dark, glass teardrops. When a volcano is active, huge drifts of Pele's glossy brown hair form on the landscape around it, like spun sugar.

BLACK SHALE

Black shales started off as gooey **mud** on the seabed. This goo formed during episodes referred to as "ocean **anoxic** events." *Anoxic* means "no oxygen," and during these events, the oceans lose oxygen and the sea life dies—although fish can't breathe air, they depend on oxygen dissolved in water to survive.

Over the long history of life on Earth, there have been five mass extinctions. These all happened many millions of years ago, but each one coincided with an ocean anoxic event. One of the most significant started 380 million years ago—known as the Late Devonian Extinction.

The word *extinction* makes it sound quick, but the process took 25 million years! In evolutionary terms, this extinction happened just after the very first vertebrates slithered onto land: The lungfish appeared in the Early Devonian epoch. Most sophisticated life forms in this period were still living in water. The rulers of these prehistoric oceans were a class of heavily armored fish known as placoderms, and the greatest of these was the *Dunkleosteus* (pronounced dunk-l-oz-tea-us), which grew up to 30 ft in length—almost as long as a school bus! A thick helmet of bony plates protected its head, and a terrifying set of jaws made its bite as powerful as a great white shark.

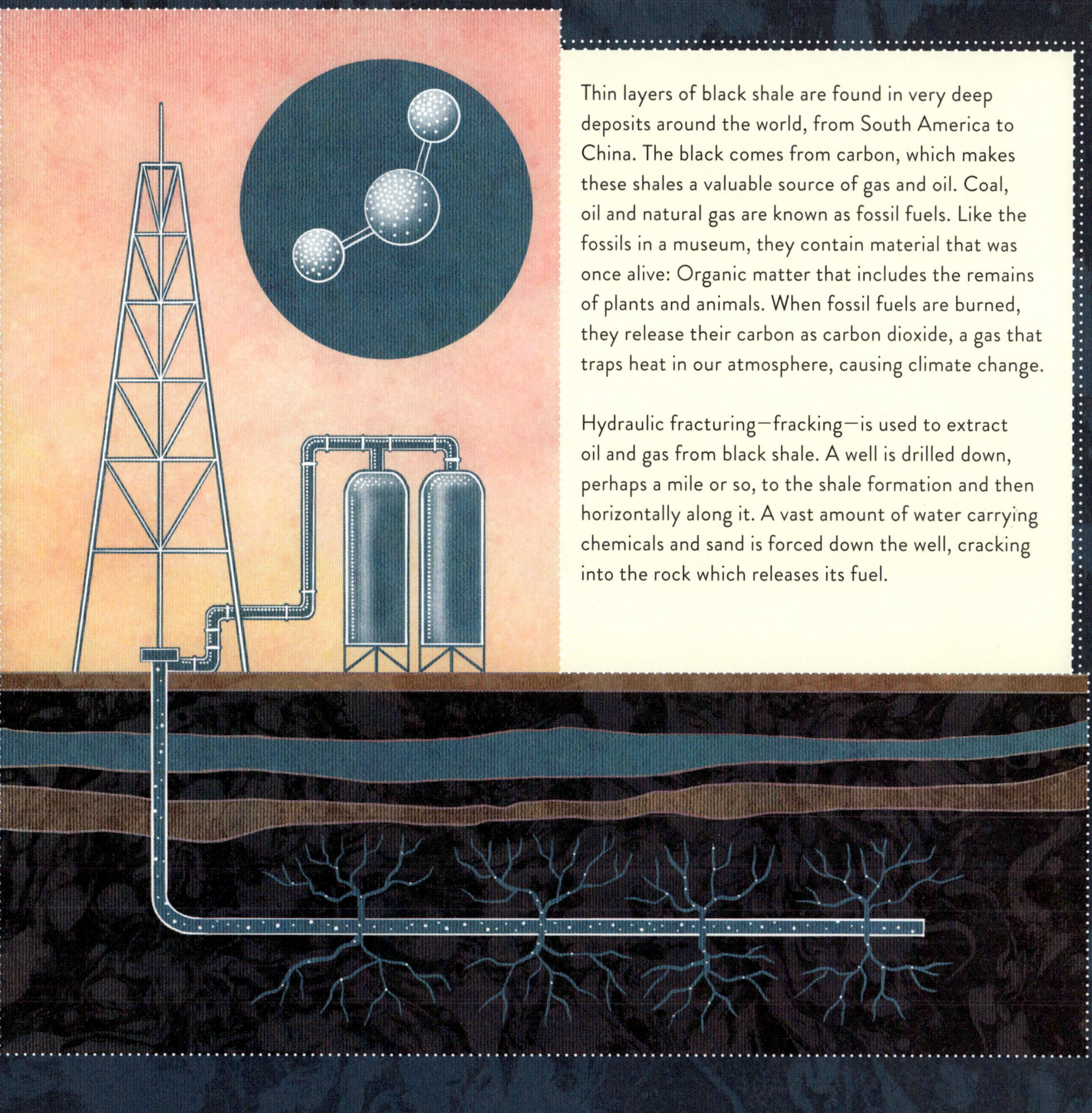

Thin layers of black shale are found in very deep deposits around the world, from South America to China. The black comes from carbon, which makes these shales a valuable source of gas and oil. Coal, oil and natural gas are known as fossil fuels. Like the fossils in a museum, they contain material that was once alive: Organic matter that includes the remains of plants and animals. When fossil fuels are burned, they release their carbon as carbon dioxide, a gas that traps heat in our atmosphere, causing climate change.

Hydraulic fracturing—fracking—is used to extract oil and gas from black shale. A well is drilled down, perhaps a mile or so, to the shale formation and then horizontally along it. A vast amount of water carrying chemicals and sand is forced down the well, cracking into the rock which releases its fuel.

The reason for the ocean anoxic events remains a mystery. They might have been caused by an enormous volcano, an asteroid, a cloak of algae blocking light to the ocean, climate change caused by the first land plants, or perhaps a combination of these things. During the Late Devonian Extinction, three-quarters of all plant and animal species were wiped out, their remains sinking to the ocean depths where they built up in mucky layers of sediment that would, over millions of years, form black shales.

Chalk

Have you ever drawn with a stick of **white** chalk? The chalk that comes in a package was probably made in a factory, but chalk is also a natural material—a variety of a sedimentary rock called **limestone**. It formed in deep beds, building up over the course of 35 million years. The white cliffs on the southeast coast of England and northwest coast of France are chalk. The stone continues to run under the landscape for hundreds of miles on either side—through France's famous Champagne region, where the grape vines are grown on soil above the chalk, then all the way up to the Baltic sea, where chalk cliffs can be seen on the coasts of Germany and Denmark.

In some places, chalk formations are many hundreds of feet thick! It is extraordinary to think that all that white stone has built up from the microscopic shells and skeletons of tiny ancient plankton. The white dust that you get on your fingers when handling chalk was once part of miniscule sea creatures that lived in a clear tropical ocean more than 66 million years ago.

Early Britons carved away the grass and soft earth to expose the white stone beneath, creating marks in the landscape that could be seen for miles. Chalk was soft and could also be packed into mounds and small hills to create tombs and other monuments that shone bright in the landscape. Sometimes they carved enormous pictures into the chalk.

The oldest surviving chalk picture in the English landscape is the 3,000-year-old Uffington White Horse in Oxfordshire. The horse has survived because the people who live nearby have looked after it carefully for all those thousands of years. The shape of the horse is formed from deep trenches. Every ten or twenty years, the trenches are cleaned and then packed with new chalk which is hammered into position to keep it from being rinsed away by the rain.

Over the centuries, certain people have looked at the chalk pictures carved into the landscape and decided they needed to be improved. There is a 236 ft high chalk picture of a man holding two poles known as the Long Man of Wilmington that is carved into a hill in Sussex. His feet used to point in opposite directions, but the Victorians decided that this looked wrong, so they recarved the Long Man so that his feet both pointed in the same direction! During the Second World War, the Long Man of Wilmington was covered up so that enemy bombers couldn't use him to find their way as they flew over the south of England.

The Latin word for chalk is *creta*. Chalk gives its name to the Cretaceous period (pronounced cre-tay-shus), which began 145 million years ago. Sixty-six million years ago, the Cretaceous period ended with a BANG when a massive asteroid hit Mexico and powerful volcanic activity erupted in western India. The end of the Cretaceous period was also the end of the dinosaurs (except for those dinosaurs that evolved to become birds). The chalk marks a boundary in the history of the Earth between the age of the dinosaurs and the rise of the mammals.

Blue Lias

Blue Lias is a thick **limestone** and **shale** rock formation found in southwest England. You can see it along the high cliffs around the town of Lyme Regis in Devon, UK. The rock is dark **gray** and made up of distinct layers—the name means "blue layers" in the old local dialect. This is sedimentary rock, built up from gunk and silt at the bottom of the sea during the Jurassic period between 195 and 210 million years ago.

Back then, Earth was home to colossal dinosaurs, among them *Diplodocus*, *Brachiosaurus* and *Allosaurus*. The oceans were populated with sponges, corals, snails, and squid, as well as enormous sea reptiles. Among these were the long-necked *Plesiosaurus*. The largest variety of *Plesiosaurus* grew up to 43 ft long (that's about the length of seven grown-ups lying in a long line!). Ichthyosaurs looked closer to a modern porpoise, with a powerful rounded body, long snout full of sharp teeth, and large eyes that helped them hunt and escape from larger predators.

The cliffs around Lyme Regis are famous for their marine fossils. During the Jurassic period, the bodies of dead sea creatures would have come to rest in the soft silt at the bottom of the ocean, where their bones, shells, and other structures were preserved in position by accumulating layers. When the cliffs around Lyme Regis crumble, sometimes they expose the fossilized remains of ancient sea creatures. If you walk along the beach, you can clearly see swirly ammonite shells stuck in the rock, but very occasionally, something much more exciting emerges!

The world's first identified *Ichthyosaurus* fossil was found by twelve-year-old Mary Anning and her older brother Joseph in 1811.

Joseph found a big skull that he couldn't identify, and Mary searched the area for remains of the creature's body, which she carefully mapped out, excavating the outline over a period of many months.

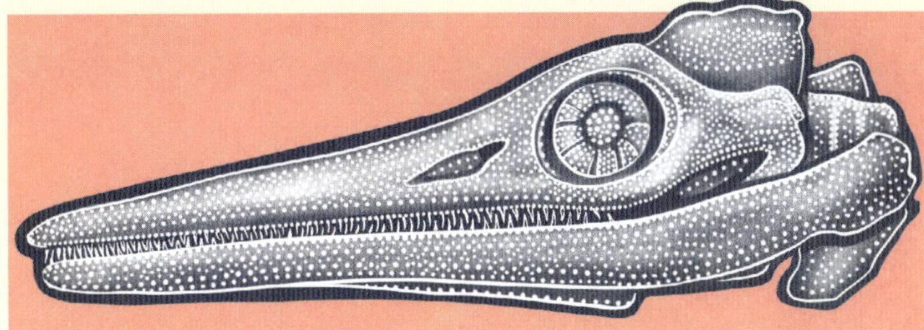

It was more than 16 ft long and, at the time, was believed to be a creature from another country, such as a crocodile!

Scientists named the fossil creature *Ichthyosaurus*, which means "fish lizard," though we now know that it was actually an ancient marine reptile. Mary Anning's discovery was important in helping scientists of the time piece together ideas about the planet and how life on it had changed.

Mary became an expert in the Blue Lias and was quick to spot unusual shapes emerging from the cliffs after storms. She trained herself to understand the anatomy of sea creatures by dissecting cuttlefish, and large flat fish called skate.

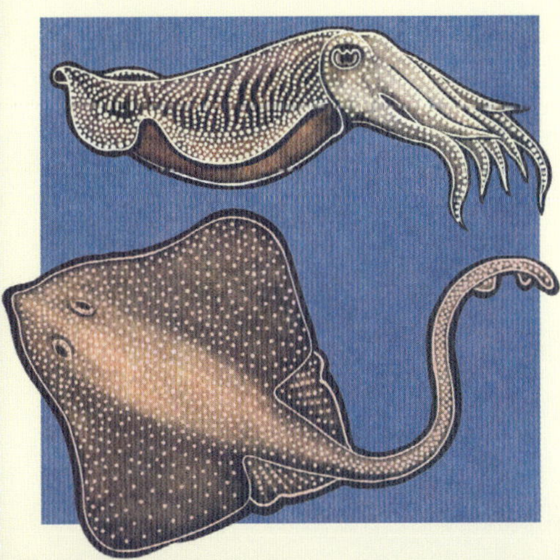

In 1823, she discovered the first fossil skeleton of a *Plesiosaurus*—its long-necked shape was so surprising that many people thought it was a fake! Some of the most important scientists of the time defended Mary Anning and confirmed that her find was real.

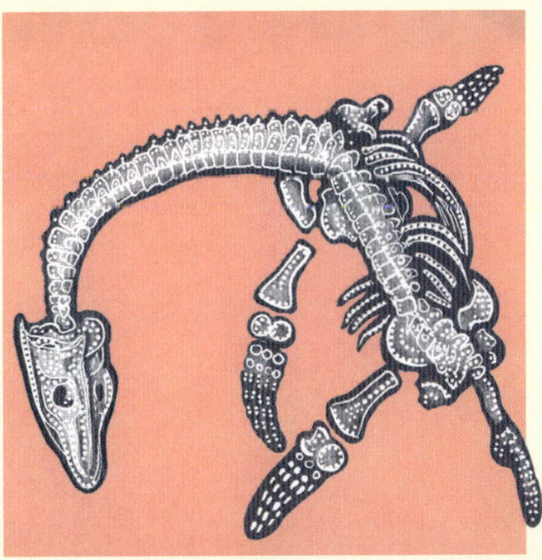

A statue of Mary Anning stands on the coast at Lyme Regis, honoring her contribution to the science now known as palaeontology. A variety of *Ichthyosaurus* that Mary discovered in 1836 has also been named in her memory: *Ichthyosaurus anningae*.

Pearl

While most gems are mined from the earth, pearls have a very different origin—they are formed by shellfish of the oyster family. The **hard** pearl is created as a defense mechanism, protecting the soft shellfish from irritants such as parasitic worms. The outer skin of the oyster produces a substance known as mother-of-pearl. If you have ever gone beachcombing, you have probably seen mother-of-pearl—it's the **glossy** material inside mussel and oyster shells. When the oyster is invaded by an irritant it covers it in mother-of-pearl. This is a way of keeping it from damaging the shellfish further.

The longer the pearl stays in the oyster, the more layers of mother-of-pearl are added and the larger it gets. Natural pearls are rare, and very few pearls from wild oysters get to the size where they can be worn as jewelry. Occasionally, however, multiple pearls are found in the same oyster! Other shellfish, such as the giant conch (a sea snail), can also form hard, round masses. Because the giant conch doesn't produce mother-of-pearl, these are dull and not prized like true pearls.

Pearls are so rare and so valuable that for many centuries, people have been searching for ways to force oysters to produce them. In 1916, a Japanese pearl farmer named Kokichi Mikimoto finally developed a method that produced perfect round, glossy pearls from farmed oysters. Mikimoto's pearls were much less expensive than wild pearls. During the 1920s and 1930s, long strings of pearls became very fashionable. Today, almost all pearls used in jewelry are farmed using the method developed by Mikimoto.

The Romans prized pearls produced by freshwater mussels in England and by oysters in the Persian Gulf. Two thousand years ago, there was already an international trade network for pearls that stretched from Britain to Sri Lanka!

Five hundred years ago, lustrous white pearls were associated with purity. Queen Elizabeth I had pearls stitched into her hair and all over her robes. All those pearls delivered an unspoken message to her important visitors: They made Elizabeth look pure and religious, and at the same time, rich and powerful.

Elizabeth I set the fashions in the royal court, so noblemen and women wanted to cover their hair and robes in pearls too. In 1585, an earl named Henry Percy spent more than £1,000 on jewelry, including 440 pearls to stitch into his clothes. Elizabeth I passed a law to make sure that only the top aristocrats could wear pearls.

Pearls of irregular shape are known as "baroque" (pronounced ba-roke) pearls. In seventeenth-century Europe, they were prized for pendants—designers used them to form the bodies of dolphins, mermaids, and mythical creatures. This era was known for a flamboyant decorative style, which became known by the same name as the oddly shaped pearls: baroque.

Basalt

Basalt is an **igneous** rock (pronounced ig-knee-us). This tough **dark** rock starts life as fiery volcanic **lava**. As the lava cools and hardens, it forms basalt. Occasionally, basalt cracks as it cools and forms dramatic many-sided columns—some can be seen at Giant's Causeway on the coast of Northern Ireland. The six-sided basalt columns look like they were carved by machines, but in fact their shapes are natural.

Earth is constantly changing, with new rock being formed. The basalt forming at rifts in the ocean is some of the youngest rock on our planet.

Basalt forms the bedrock of two-thirds of the surface of the Earth, but most of that area is underwater. Deep beneath the sand and sediment, our oceans are lined in basalt about 3 mi thick. It was not until the 1950s that scientists first started to map the ocean floor in detail. The ocean gets very deep indeed, so scientists couldn't just swim down and take measurements. Instead, the American geologists Bruce Heezen and Marie Tharp analyzed SONAR readings, which use sound to measure distance and detect shapes in the water.

Through the SONAR readings, Heezen and Tharp discovered that there was a submerged mountain range right in the middle of the Atlantic Ocean! This enormous underwater mountain range is sliced all the way down by a valley. Tharp suggested that this valley was a rift—a split in the Earth's crust caused by movement of tectonic plates. The plates move apart by a few inches every year, and as they do, molten rock rises into the gap and cools to form basalt. This process has been going on for a long time: The basalt nearest to the rift is quite newly formed, but as you travel away from the rift toward the continents on either side of the Atlantic, the basalt is 100 million years old.

It's not only ancient people that have built enormous monuments out of earth and stone. Modern artists have made them, too! Some of the most famous artists to make land art were husband and wife Robert Smithson and Nancy Holt. The biggest monument they worked on is named Spiral Jetty. It was constructed in 1970 on the Great Salt Lake in Utah, in an area where the lake water has been turned plum pink by bacteria. Spiral Jetty is a walkway about a mile long that stretches into the lake, then coils around and around like a snail shell. It is constructed from 6,624 tons of black basalt from the shores of the lake.

Basalt contains a large quantity of iron. When it cools, magnetite forms, which shows the direction of Earth's magnetic poles at the time the basalt formed. Thanks to these crystals inside the basalt, scientists testing the floor of the Atlantic Ocean discovered something absolutely mind-boggling. The Earth's magnetic poles switch every 500,000 years—with north taking the place of south, and vice versa—and have done so for at least 150 million years.

Coral

Is coral animal, mineral, or vegetable? It's all three! Coral is an amazing example of symbiosis—organisms that have evolved to coexist and support one another. The tiny coral **polyp** is a relative of the jellyfish, less than 0.12 in in length. Hard varieties, such as brain or staghorn corals, are in fact colonies of hundreds of thousands of polyps, each of which constructs its own little stony home around itself. The color in coral is produced by **algae** called zooxanthellae (pronounced zoo-zan-thell-ee) that live within the cells of the coral polyp. Zooxanthellae take energy from sunlight, and they feed much of this energy back into the polyp. In return, the polyp offers the zooxanthellae the protection of their stony home and nutrients taken from drifting food particles they catch in their tentacles.

Coral's stony structure is built from calcium carbonate—so coral is a form of limestone. The remains of ancient corals can be seen in limestone deposits around the world.

A coral reef is formed when many hard corals grow together in a part of the ocean that is well suited to their needs—warm, shallow, and clear enough for the sunlight to reach the zooxanthellae. They are very sensitive to changes in their environment. High temperatures, rising or falling water levels, and any kind of cloudiness or pollution can cause the coral to "bleach" and eventually die. Coral can recover from bleaching, but it takes more than ten years for them to heal and regenerate.

There are many myths about how coral formed. The Roman poet Ovid told the story of how Perseus killed Medusa, a Gorgon whose gaze turned living things to stone. After beheading Medusa, Perseus was flying away from her island when he saw a beautiful woman named Andromeda chained to the rocks, about to be eaten by a sea monster. Perseus killed the sea monster—this was a messy business, and he needed to wash before unchaining Andromeda. While he was rinsing his hands in the sea, he placed Medusa's head on a bed of seaweed. Medusa's gaze was still so powerful even after death that she turned the soft seaweed into the first stony corals.

Australia's Great Barrier Reef is the largest living structure on Earth. There are more than 600 different species of coral living there. The reef as it appears today is 10,000 years old, but there has been a coral reef system there for more than half a million years.

True to its name, the Great Barrier Reef is an incredible natural barrier, protecting the northeast coast of Australia from powerful ocean surges and waves. Indigenous peoples of the region have many stories about the origin of the reef. In one story told by the Gimuy Walubara Yidinji people, a man named Gunya was fishing with his wife. Sensing movement in the water, Gunya threw his spear. What he hit was not a tasty fish, but a sacred stingray named Morijum. Morijum was furious and flapped his mighty wings, creating huge waves that thundered toward the shore. Gunya and his wife paddled back to land and heated rocks on a fire, which they then threw into the water to calm the waves. The rocks they threw formed the Great Barrier Reef, which still protects the coast today.

Stony Secrets and Lithic Lingo

Inside the Earth

You live on the thinnest, coolest outer layer of Earth, known as the **crust**. If you could slice through our planet, you would find four sections. Each section behaves in a different way. At the center is the **inner core**, a dense ball mostly made up of iron and nickel. Although the inner core is incredibly hot (more than 9,392 °F!), pressure at the center of the Earth keeps it solid. Around it sits the liquid **outer core,** which is mostly metal. Between the crust and the core of the Earth lies the **mantle**, which is 1,800 mi thick and makes up 84 percent of our planet. The upper section of the mantle, together with the crust, form the solid outer part of Earth known as the **lithosphere**.

That's My Type of Rock!

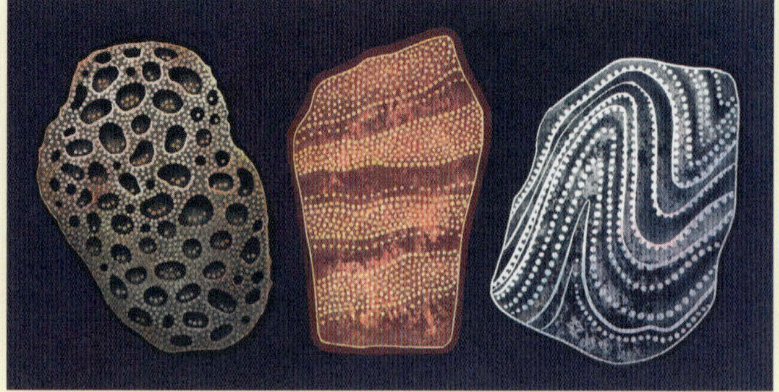

Here on the lithosphere, we are surrounded by three main types of rock. **Igneous** rock is cooled magma or lava. Granite is an igneous rock. **Sedimentary** rock is built up from small particles—these might be eroded parts of older rocks, fine mud, or the shells and bones of dead organisms. Sandstone is a sedimentary rock. **Metamorphic** rock is igneous or sedimentary rock that has been transformed by the Earth's pressure and heat. Marble is a metamorphic rock.

Lithic means "of or relating to stone."

Lithosphere means "stone globe" or "stone ball."

In Latin **igneous** means "fiery"—it is related to the word *ignite*, which means "to start burning."

Around the World with Plate Tectonics

The **lithosphere** is made up of enormous slabs known as **plates**. There are oceanic plates beneath the water and continental plates beneath the land. Under the lithosphere, the mantle is extremely hot and not completely solid. Heat released from the core of the Earth causes the hot material in the mantle to move very slowly. This in turn causes the lithosphere to move very slowly. The term ***plate tectonics*** describes how the plates of the lithosphere move. Whether in the ocean or on land, the boundary between two tectonic plates is associated with earthquakes and volcanoes.

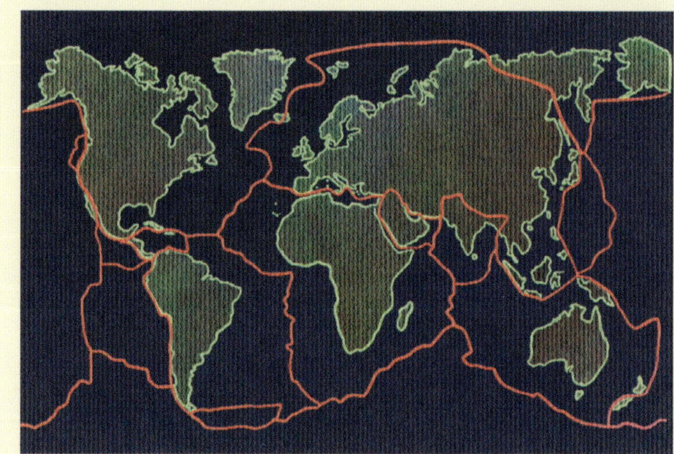

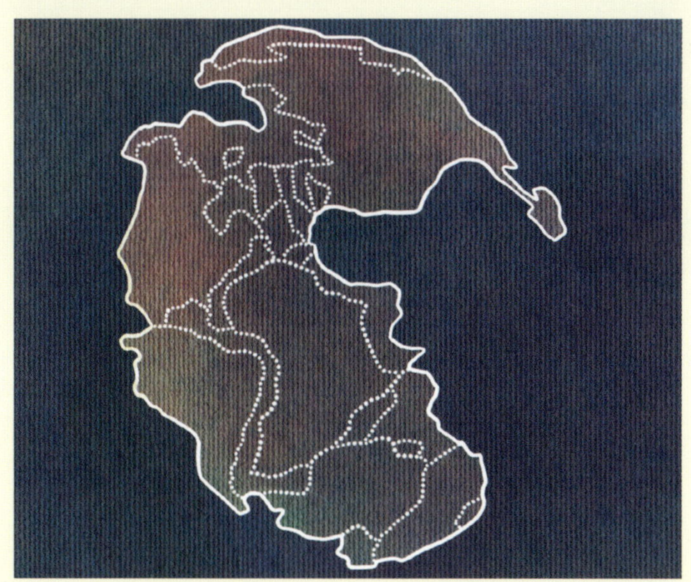

The Ancient History of Supercontinents

The first tectonic plates formed more than 3 billion years ago. Although the plates of the lithosphere move very slowly, over the course of billions of years there have been periods when the continental plates collided to form a single landmass. These enormous expanses of land are known as **supercontinents**. Scientists named the most recent supercontinent Pangaea. It would have formed incredibly slowly more than 300 million years ago. After about 100 million years, Pangaea gradually started to break up again.

Meet the Minerals

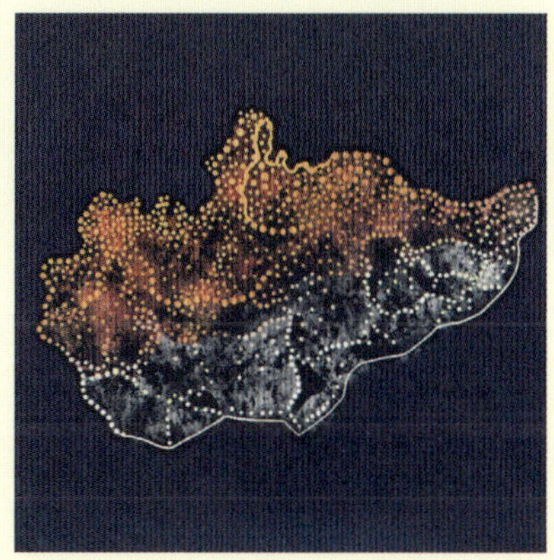

Minerals are naturally occurring solid substances with distinctive crystal structures. Different kinds of mineral are known as **mineral species**. Minerals that contain a large amount of metal are called **ores**. Some rocks contain just one mineral species, but a single type of rock can also be composed of many different minerals. For example, the minerals that make up granite include quartz, feldspar, and plagioclase. **Gemstones** such as diamonds, rubies, and emerald are all minerals prized for their beauty.

Are All Minerals Hard?

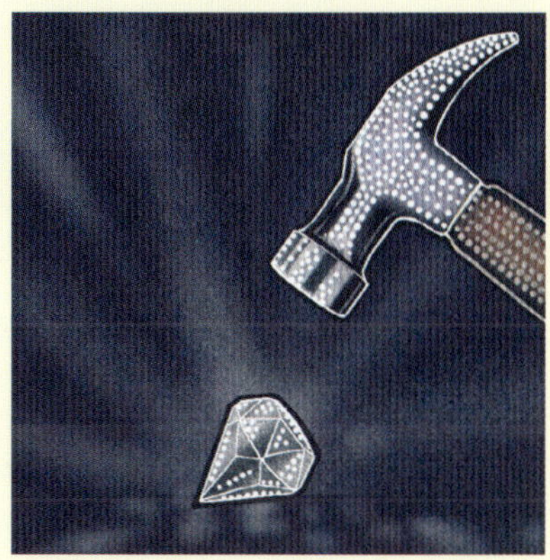

Minerals have different properties. Some, such as talc, are so soft that you can mark them with your fingernail. Minerals are measured for hardness on the **Mohs scale**—talc is at the bottom, rated 1. Minerals are arranged on the Mohs scale according to their ability to leave a scratch on the surface of a mineral of another species. At the top and rated 10 is diamond, the hardest naturally occurring substance on Earth. The scale was invented by the German geologist Friedrich Mohs in 1812.

Turning Minerals into Jewels

Gemstones in their natural state are known as **rough**. To be worn in jewelry, minerals need to be cut and polished. Through cutting and polishing, the stones are shaped and become shiny and sparkly. Gemstones such as rubies, diamonds, emeralds, and sapphires are valued according to their size, their color, and how clear they are. Most gems are clouded with faults and impurities: Clear stones sparkle more once cut. The sides of a cut gemstone are known as **facets**.

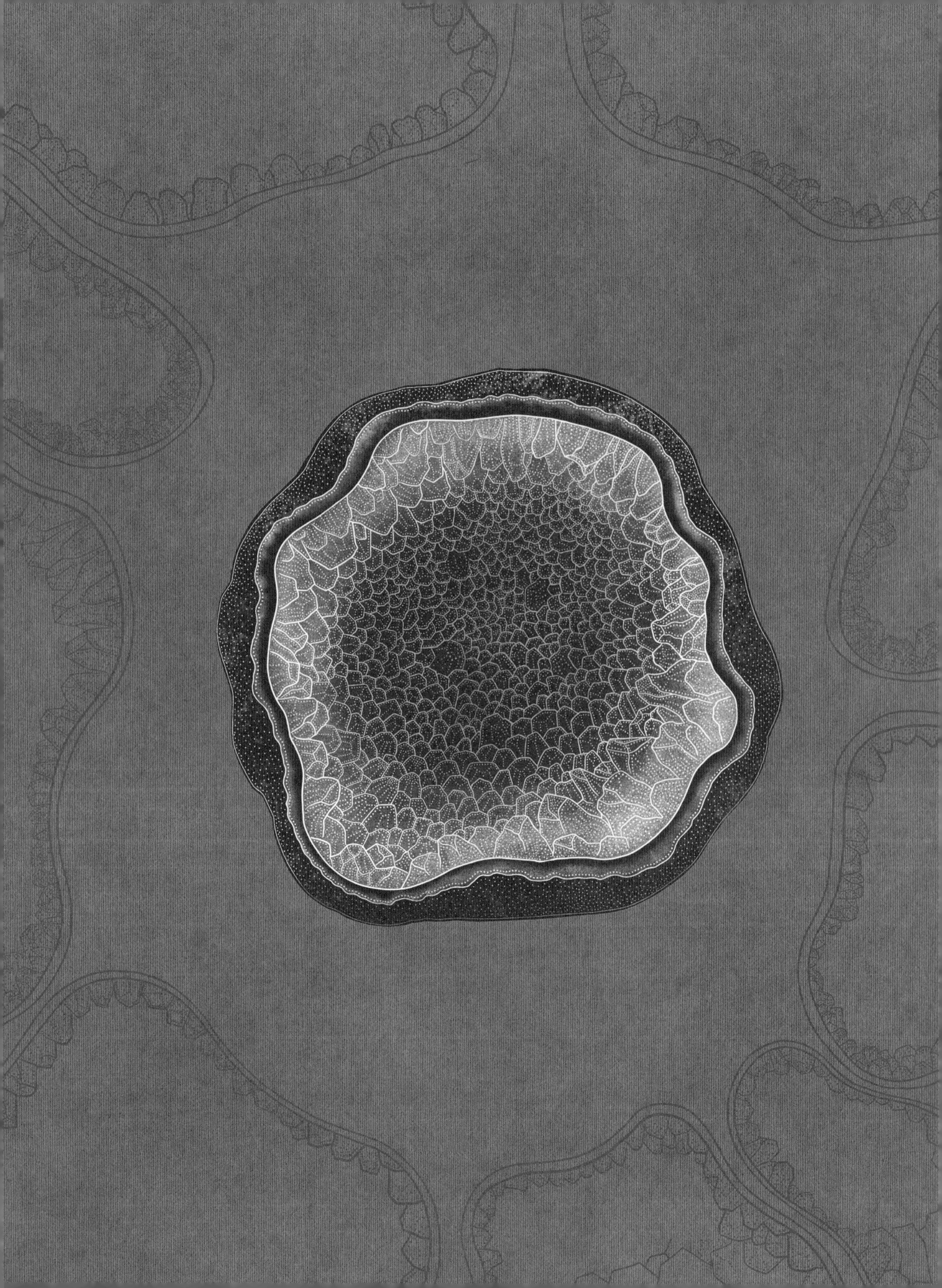